the
abbey
house

an heirloom island novel

ELIZABETH
BROMKE

In loving memory of Jody McDaniel

PROLOGUE

Some women were moved to marriage. Wired for it. They sprinted past every single notable adolescent accomplishment, irreverent to proms and high school graduation and things like jobs. They sailed into the arms of the first man who kissed them or professed his undying love or took them home to meet Mother.

You see, these were the same women who turned up in the labor and delivery ward precisely nine months after those rushed wedding vows. Sometimes, they turned up earlier, claiming a mix-up with the timeline of their last-known cycle or with the baby's growth rate.

Sometimes, they turned up at the hospital years

later, after vitamins and special exercises and praying so hard that God's ears burned.

But in the end, everything happened perfectly for some women, and indeed, they were all the more *perfect* for their perfect choices.

She was not some women, though.

She was not perfect, and she was not moved to marriage or tracking her cycle or bothering with prenatal anything. But that was before she met Hendrik. Before the money and the promises and the perfect pregnancy that came in spite of her indifference. Or, more aptly, *because* of it.

That's what Hendrik had always said. *We got pregnant because we weren't trying!* She hated that. Hated that he'd used the We're Pregnant line and We this and We that.

To her, it was a lonely thing, pregnancy. It was the loneliest thing in the whole, wide world. And that was pretty funny, really, considering the fact that she had everything that some women prayed for.

CHAPTER 1—CADENCE

THE DISCOVERY

A gull squawked and swooped low in front of the trio that had crowded together at the edge of Lake Huron.

Five more birds followed the first, and they sailed through the air and up north. Maybe toward Mackinaw or Drummond, Cadence expected. To her, birds were a bit like tourists, flocking to the best nearest attraction. To the most beautiful, most peopled area they could find. There was sure to be good pickings up north.

The gulls of Lake Huron didn't usually stick around through winter, when the water froze clear from Birch Harbor over to the eastern shore. They left for the southern seas.

Now, however, they were back, feeding from the

Great Lake and roosting there, too. Gulls were scavengers, sure. But they weren't crows or ravens.

They weren't vultures.

And even so, there was nothing left here, at the easternmost shore of Heirloom Island. There was nothing at this building site, with its shallow grave. Nothing for any bird to scavenge.

Nothing, either, for Cadence to see.

The police had already removed the evidence.

Presently, Cadence shivered, despite the season. She hugged herself, wrapping a lightweight white sweater snug over her body. The month of May could be a maddening one. Sunny and toasty one day. Then came a frigid breeze, curling around the island like Jack Frost himself.

Death, however, was a cold thing no matter the weather. No matter the season.

Cadence gave one last hard look at the soft earth beyond the yellow tape. Then, she nodded, satisfied, and returned her sunglasses to the bridge of her nose.

Darla had stayed home with the boys. No reason to drag them out on some macabre excursion.

Tatum came, though. She had brought along Angus—*just in case.* In case of what, Cadence wasn't sure. The deed had long since been done. No danger appeared to remain.

Tatum had also brought Rip. Or, more accurately, Rip had brought Tatum and Cadence. This was his project site. It was his territory.

His discovery.

But it was Cadence's problem.

CHAPTER 2—CADENCE

EARLIER THAT DAY

Cadence Van Dam pulled her vehicle into the staff parking lot, a small, hidden-away square of asphalt at the back of the school. Edging around a scarce smattering of cars already locked in for the school day loomed snow berms in various heights and shapes. Some long and low, giving a clear view of Lake Huron beyond. Some high and towering, as though the plow must have taken fits to corral all the snow it possibly could into one frozen mountain.

As though whoever had done the plowing, had children in mind.

Cadence could just picture her pupils hurrying out across the playground and to this very back lot to shave into place the perfect sledding hill.

She parked, eased into the cold air and

walked back to the trunk, retrieving her coat and the canvas tote in which she kept a leather folio, a sack lunch, and little extras she'd use over the course of a school day. Gum. Lipstick. A hairbrush. Spare gloves on the good chance she'd get the pair she was wearing *wet*. Nothing was worse than being cold and wet, and it was the one part of winter Cadence didn't much care for.

It was the part of winter that brought out her longing for May. For spring. For the promise of summer and a stretch of warmth that carried her back into a new school year.

But this current day was duly frozen over, and in truth—anything that happened to get wet would likely freeze back up just as soon, anyway.

Cadence pulled on her coat and slipped an arm through the looping hands of her tote, closed the trunk, and started for the school building.

St. Mary's school was directly adjacent to St. Mary's parish. The various buildings on the campus all matched neatly. An outsider wouldn't know the family hall from the junior high wing. The uniformity comforted Cadence.

Of course, the church building itself stood out, what with a pearl-white archway peppered in stained glass and pearl-white columns that drove themselves up into heaven itself.

Cadence followed the pretty brick building along past classroom windows until she arrived at the main entrance, the boxy front building that housed the school offices, the rectory, and the mailroom.

She walked with a purpose through the front doors, over outdated green carpet, and directly into the headmaster's office of St. Mary's Catholic School.

Once inside but before Mr. McGee had even noticed her presence, Cadence shrugged off her faux-fur-lined winter coat, draped it over the same arm upon which she wore her tote, then shifted all her weight onto her left hip.

Then Cadence tapped her faux-fur-trimmed snow boot. She didn't bother with a greeting for Mr. McGee. Instead, she dove right in. "We need to talk."

He looked up from his computer at last, as befuddled by her interruption as he'd likely been with whatever online endeavor he'd previously been pursuing. "Hrm?" Then he gave his head a clearing shake. "Mrs. Van Dam. *Ms.*," he quickly corrected. Ever since Hendrik's death, people had gotten a little funny about titles. Mostly, Cadence was offended to be treated as though she'd never even been married.

But time was helping her accept that social

graces didn't always account for things like Mrs. or Ms. in the wake of one's husband's death.

She took the liberty of pulling out one of two wood-backed chairs that sat opposite him. Lowering into it, she lay her coat and tote across her lap and let out a sigh. "Mr. McGee. Have you heard? About the new school?"

"The new school?" He scratched his bald spot. Could a headmaster *be* any more of a caricature? Cadence thought not. "No?"

It was the first day back from Christmas vacation, and Cadence's very presence at St. Mary's should be a bit of a shock to the man. Their last conversation covered whether Cadence would return for the spring term at all. She'd been hoping to become Darla's full-time nanny.

But things change. People change. Minds change.

And new schools get chartered.

From her tote, Cadence pulled out an envelope, inside of which was a detailed mission and vision statement. Also, a school charter for The New Traditional School of the Great Lakes, signed Dr. Roger K. Rutherford, sub-signed Mr. Vance D. Chamberlain. Dated the October prior. "Here." She smoothed the thick packet of academia verbiage on Mr. McGee's desk. "See for yourself."

He pulled it his way and adjusted his bifocals, reading with such intensity that Cadence began to feel even worse about the whole situation. Even a little scared, maybe.

After several long moments, Mr. McGee finally pulled his glasses to the tip of his nose and assessed Cadence with the new knowledge. "Well, then. This is..." He tapped a single finger on his desktop. "...Concerning."

"Concerning," Cadence echoed. "I hate to be redundant, but I'm an active participant in the board meetings. I know our numbers, Mr. McGee. I know St. Mary's is slipping."

"Our enrollment dropped by fifteen percent this year alone. Families want opportunity. Not religion." He clicked his tongue and shook his head. "We can't compete." He folded the packet back into its thirds and returned it to the envelope.

"What? You're just—you're just giving up?" Cadence made a face and took the damnable thing back from him.

He gave a shrug. "I'm not giving up, but it's not something within our control. The secular education system, I mean. Public school. It's—well, we just can't compete, like I said, Ms. Van Dam."

"This—" Cadence flapped the envelope in the air, "is hardly a public school. It's a charter school. Technically public, yes, but their proposal presents a model that isn't so dissimilar from what we're doing here, Mr. McGee. A traditional education. Conservative values. Small class sizes and a values-based education."

He cleared his throat. "How did this come to your attention?"

Cadence wanted to ask how it *had not* come to his. Instead, she replied gently, "A local mentioned it. I suppose it made the paper."

"The *Herald*?" He scratched his head again, but it was no use. He had no new ideas, apparently. "Well. I don't know what to tell you, Cadence."

She was astounded at his veritable indifference. "What if we make an effort? A push, you know?"

"An effort to what? Recruit more students? Where will they come from? Heirloom Island is not exactly a flourishing metropolis, Cadence." He said all of this gently, and it was all true.

"Where do you think this charter is bringing students in from?"

"Birch Harbor, sure. But only a fraction will

make that journey." Mr. McGee pulled off his glasses and cleaned them with a square of fabric. "Unfortunately, I doubt this new school will have any success. We're an island. We're isolated by our very nature. And while St. Mary's serves many of the families here on Heirloom, it doesn't serve all. We continue to lose families to the bigger townships on the mainland. The ones with sports and clubs and laptops. Ms. Van Dam, I just don't see how a small parochial school can contend." He looked helpless, but Cadence couldn't fathom St. Mary's ceasing to be. Not only was it a historic locale on the Island and in the county, it was where Cadence genuinely believed her life began. Her first teaching job. Her first love.

"Well, that's why I'm here, Mr. McGee. We can contend, and we will. If a small, traditional charter school can get up on its legs on the island, then we can get back on our feet, too."

He didn't look convinced.

Cadence persisted. "We're going to have an open house. If not to draw back those pupils who might consider charter, then to woo new students. Maybe there are families on the island with upcoming kindergarteners. Maybe they don't know much about our school. Maybe, too, we have new people on the island. Educating people about their education options can be powerful."

He bowed his head and drummed his fingers on his desk a few beats before slipping his glasses back up his nose and looking at Cadence. "If you think you can pull off an open house, Father Richard, the board, and I would all appreciate that greatly. We can't offer much in the way of resources, you know—"

But Cadence was already out of her seat and pulling her tote back up to her shoulder, a million ideas coursing through her brain like a pinwheel. "Thank you!"

Now, she just had to convince her sisters to help her.

CHAPTER 3—DARLA

Darla wanted to cling to Christmas break. With all of her might. She wanted the tree left up. She wanted hot cocoa every morning, with marshmallows bubbling up on top. She wanted to cuddle her boys well into late morning and feed them whenever they needed milk. She didn't want to establish a schedule.

Not yet.

Yet, by the first week of January, Darla would have to. She was due back at the school. She'd said she was going to return. She *wanted* to return. But that was then.

This is now.

Darla's mind had changed. She'd settled into motherhood. In a matter of weeks, she'd gone from being sleep deprived and scared to sleep deprived and happy. Euphoric, even. Darla had predicted a lot of things about motherhood. She'd predicted contentment and routine and a sense of purpose. She'd predicted she'd like it, being a mother. She hadn't predicted that it would fulfill her entirely. That she'd come to believe she'd never need anything ever again. Not her own home, not a husband. Not even the career she'd built her life around.

And so, the Friday before returning, she'd done the unthinkable. Darla had called Mr. McGee at St. Mary's and dropped a bomb. She wasn't coming back. She needed more time. Cadence could cover her classes until they found someone permanent to take over her position.

It was, in truth, the easiest *No* Darla had ever delivered.

So, there she was, the first Monday of the second semester, bleary and blissful, with two babies snuggled against her chest as she lay in bed watching *Good Morning Lake Huron*. Could life get any better?

Well, yes.

Life would be better if she could make money without actually reporting to work in any way, shape, or form. It was the only niggling fleck of stress in her brain. Cadence had assured Darla that they'd work on the venue and events business. That she'd keep working, of course, and they'd scrape by. Anyway, they had the rental. That was passive income. Everything would work out, Cadence had said.

And then, she'd left for work.

Darla slid herself out of bed, tucking each twin into his bassinet as carefully as possible, so as not to wake them. Then she pulled on a terry cloth robe and crept down the stairs.

Cadence had left coffee brewing and bowls ready with rolled oats.

Darla wondered if Tatum had stayed at the shelter the night before. She'd become unreliable in her presence at the boardwalk house. More often than not, she stayed at The Manger House with the animals. In fact, to Darla's memory, Tatum's last night at their shared home on the lake was days earlier.

Darla filled a mug with coffee—hot chocolate was more of a pipe dream when one was *this* tired. Then she set about boiling milk for the oats as she shuffled through notifications on her phone.

Cadence wished her a happy first day as a stay-at-home mom. Darla smiled.

Nothing from Tatum. Typical. She rarely had her phone on her.

Feeling the pang of lonesomeness, Darla scrolled further in her text messages, until she came upon the one name she couldn't seem to shake. Mason.

They'd been forced into contact, of course. He'd come to the opening of the animal shelter. He'd helped Tatum. He'd helped Darla, too, move back into the house with her sister. But that was it. Darla remained as frigid as she could, and that was pretty frigid. Postpartum hormones were nothing to sneeze at, and there wasn't one little speck of an urge to talk to Mason. Not *that* way, at least.

But even hormones couldn't erase the fact that Darla enjoyed Mason's company. He made her laugh and smile. They were friends. They were only ever friends, of course. And that foundation—the friendship—couldn't just go away. Friendship wasn't always a verb, as Darla sometimes had told her students. Sometimes, friendship was simply a truth. A fact. And with Mason, it seemed like she couldn't deny the truth—the fact—of his friendship.

Milk started bubbling on the stove as Darla's thumb hovered over their last conversation. She tapped it.

An empty space for a fresh message sat at the

bottom of her phone screen. Darla set the device down and turned off the stove. She poured her oats into the pot and stirred absently.

After a few moments letting her breakfast cook up then cool down, she transferred it to the bowl Cadence had set out, then carried her coffee and oatmeal to the table. She wasn't going to eat there. She ate in bed, near the boys while the TV kept her company.

Her breakfast now waiting on the table, Darla returned to the bar, scooped up her phone and stared again at the blank bar at the bottom.

She chewed her lip, gripped the device in both hands, and went for it.

"Hi! How've you been? Just writing to say hi and check in. I'm home with the boys this semester and just happened to think of you," she wrote. Then she deleted it. It was a little personal, right? Too intimate? Desperate? Long-winded? She thought about what he *was* doing today, which she knew. She knew, because Mason was a teacher, too. Just like Darla and Cadence. He taught on the mainland at the high school. Music. She thought about the fact that he'd get ready every morning in a houseboat and take his truck to school to sing songs with teenagers, and it all made Darla feel unreasonably jealous. Not of Mason.

Of the teenagers.

She started her message. "Hope you have a great semester! If you're free this weekend, I'd love to catch up!" She stared at the second sentence, amazed at her own brazenness. Or was it cowardice? Going back on one's plans, one's values. That had to be cowardice. She planted her thumb on the back-space icon, ready to forget it all, but just when she did, a throaty wail came from upstairs. Gabriel. She knew it well.

Startled now, Darla forgot entirely about the message, dropped her phone on the table with her breakfast and made for the stairs. She took them two at a time—a great postpartum workout—and arrived at Gabriel's bassinet. His little face was pinched and red. Darla scooped him up deftly and took him for a change before Shep could wake, too —it was a miracle he hadn't yet.

An hour and two diaper changes later, Darla finally made her way, twins in their carrier on her chest, back down to her breakfast. It was cold, of course, but she didn't mind. She was famished enough to devour most of it, including downing the coffee before deciding to set out for a walk.

It was then, when she grabbed her phone to get packed and bundled up to head out, that she remembered her ridiculous, fleeting lonesomeness and the text she was going to send.

Only, it wasn't there, sitting in that blank bar at the bottom of her screen once she woke her phone up. The message Darla was *going to send*—actually, the message Darla was *going* to erase, especially now that she'd shaken that stupid, transitory moment of weakness.

Before her eyes, just as the boys cooed against their mother's chest in their booties and hats and mittens, those three undulating dots appeared beneath Darla's message.

Mason was replying.

CHAPTER 4—TATUM

Things were coming together nicely at The Manger House. With Rip's help, Tatum had transformed one of the old farmhouse bedrooms into her own bedroom, complete with a restored iron-frame double bed, a refinished wardrobe, and a nightstand.

The rest of the house, which now made for a great live-in business, was steadily improving, too. The heating, plumbing, and even air conditioning systems were all a go—the nice thing about dating a contractor, Tatum came to realize.

But *were* they dating? This was the big question.

Rip arrived that morning with two steaming to-go cups of Hot Diddly Scrumptious from the Koken. Tatum had discovered this drink that winter and going even a day without it was beginning to give her the shakes.

"I don't know what I did to deserve home-delivered hot cocoa on a Monday morning, but whatever it was—I'll keep on doing it."

Rip kissed her cheek and passed over her cup. Angus ambled to the door, ready for pets from his second-favorite human. The other dogs would be along soon, as would Selena, the cat.

He squatted down until he was sitting fully on the hallway runner and the whole gang was licking his face and dangerously close to slurping up his drink. Tatum took Rip's and laughed, happy as a loon, before carrying them both into the kitchen, where she'd set out a simple breakfast for the both of them.

Rip had a busy day ahead, but he was never too busy to swing by the shelter. If not to visit Tatum then to get his furry cuddles. It's one of the many things Tatum loved about the guy. Or, maybe one of the many things that she *liked* about him. Okay, well, *loved*. You could *love* something about someone without loving the person, right? Because Tatum still couldn't be sure about what she felt for Rip. And she definitely didn't know what he felt for her.

And again, were they *even* dating?

She studied him as he sat and gobbled down quick-mix pancakes topped in butter and dripping with syrup. Tatum liked a man who wasn't fussy with his food, because Tatum wasn't fussy either. Two unfussy people felt like the closest thing to love a gal could get. She shook the thought.

"So, you're back on that project this week, right? The school?" Tatum sat and dug into a second helping of pancakes herself. As hectic as it was opening a new business and running the island's only animal shelter, she hadn't established a good eating routine. So when she did sit down to a real meal, she made it count.

"Yeah." He gave her a look. Despite the fact that Cadence and Darla had made their feelings known on the topic of the school, Tatum decided to toe the line a little more carefully. It wasn't her fault *or* Rip's fault that he was profiting off the establishment of a new school.

Anyway, Rip felt pretty bad about the whole thing. He'd even been dragging his feet. He'd admitted as much privately to Tatum. *I don't want to mess things up*, he'd confessed quietly one day as they were painting the barn one sunny-cold afternoon, *but I'm not going to push matters.*

She'd asked him what he meant.

We can't work when it's actively snowing, so there's that. And if we've got heavy snow on the ground, it's a complication.

Tatum had reminded him he couldn't change the weather. So if the weather was delaying the build, that wasn't Rip dragging his hands.

We've pushed through bad weather before, Tatum. He was a little guilty-acting about that, maybe. *We could push through this.*

But in the end he stuck to the protocol: wait until snow has melted down and the forecast was clear. And that had put Rip starting at precisely the first week of the second school semester. The timing worked well enough because it meant employees of St. Mary's wouldn't be around to bug Rip or his workers or the fellow who'd commissioned the build —a one Dr. Roger K. Rutherford. Tatum had committed the name to memory because ever since the opening party and Cadence had learned about the new school, she'd used the man's name like she might use a swear word. Irregularly, but with such venom and propulsion that Tatum couldn't exactly forget it.

Rip continued to eat, and Tatum did, too. Once they'd both finished, bellies full and dogs chomping at the bit for dregs of syrup, Tatum glanced at the clock. "What time do you need to be there?"

He looked at his watch, which was funny. Whenever you asked anyone what time they needed to be somewhere, they always seemed to refer to a clock or a watch as if it had the final authority on the person's schedule. Well, it kind of did. Rip sighed. "Half an hour."

"Need any company?" she offered. Tatum wasn't one to put herself out there for others and Rip had to know this by now. Surely he realized she *wanted* to go with him.

"What, you mean you're going to let me take Angus?" He scrubbed beneath the old dog's collar.

Tatum frowned. "No. I mean—" But her thought was suspended by the fact that he *did not* realize she wanted to go with him. "Well. Okay. If you want him to go. He can go." She folded her arms and gave the dog a look that a mother would give a teenage boy. *Behave.*

Rip laughed, though, and took both their plates to the sink, dunking them in the dishwater. "I'm kidding, Tate."

She rounded her lips over to the side and joined him there with a towel, ready to dry. When she did, he gently bumped her with his hip. "Don't you have intakes or something going on today?"

"You don't want me to go?" She avoided looking his way and instead focused on drying every last drop from between the tines of a fork.

"I'd love for you to come, but not at the sacrifice of your work."

"It's not really *work*." Oh, no. Tatum was already doing it. Already being weird about spending time with Rip. She pursed her lips. "You're right, actually. I have a lot to do." She made her eyes go wide and clicked her tongue. "A *lot*."

His face fell, she was almost positive it did. "Welp." He scratched the back of his neck. "Do you think I can steal you away for lunch?"

A smile sprang up from Tatum's insides and painted her face in bright pink. "Steal me? You can *have* me." But it came out awkward and wrong, and Rip laughed, and Tatum's bright pink happy flush turned to a deep red mortification. "I mean—"

"I know." He planted his hands on her waist and pulled her in for a light kiss on the lips. Rip always seemed to taste like he'd just been out chopping wood. Not sweaty. Musky. Manly. Woodsy. She liked it. She felt the blood drain back down her neck and settle once more into her heart and pump through the rest of her body, as it ought to have.

"Noon?"

"I don't think I can wait that long. How about eleven?"

The morning crept by at a sleepy puppy's pace. Then, the next thing Tatum knew, it was half past ten and she hadn't so much as run a comb through her hair. Of course, Rip had already seen her in her PJs and sans makeup, but if they were going to lunch —or even just eating sandwiches at the project site —she wanted to look pretty. This meant a swipe of lipstick and a tidy ponytail. Maybe a pair of earrings. A scarf? Should she wear her going-out boots or snow boots? She peeked out the window of the kitchen. The snow was all but gone, only patches remained. She could definitely get away with the going-out boots.

Tatum scurried to her bedroom, animals in tow, to hurry and get ready, but before she so much as pulled on a fresh sweater, her cell phone rang from somewhere in the house. Tatum rarely kept the dang thing on her. She wasn't like most women her age.

She didn't sleep with the phone. She didn't keep it shoved in a back pocket or neatly packed in the front pocket of her purse. And it certainly didn't find itself sewn to her hand like an appendage.

But, Tatum *had* gotten better about answering it. Now that Darla had the boys and all three sisters were more or less dependent upon one another, Tatum learned that answering their texts and calls was part and parcel of a strong sisterhood, no matter how annoying Tatum thought cell phones, generally speaking, were.

There was one other reason to keep it charged, though.

Rip, naturally.

Tatum dug around her bedsheets, as if she might find it there. But the sound didn't grow louder with the toss and flip of each layer. She scrambled through the house, searching the kitchen table and counters. The phone gave one last ring, and it wasn't any louder, either. Then, it stopped.

A moment later, the familiar chime of a voice-mail. *Drat*, Tatum thought, edgily. Now she'd never find it.

She did her best to rush through the rest of her preparations—getting dressed, adding the lipstick and pulling back her hair. Then she needed to let the dogs out. Then she needed to do a walk-through of the barn. She currently had three tenants out there. Two dogs and one goat. All fine.

At last, Tatum was ready to leave, but it was after eleven. She was late. Or Rip was.

Then again, was he supposed to pick her up? Or was she meeting him? Or was she picking *him* up from his project site? Tatum had no recollection, and now she realized the phone call she'd missed was probably Rip sorting that out.

She made her way back into the house, riling up the dogs and Serena all over again, as she searched the place for the umpteenth time. Or, technically the second time. But an exhaustive second time, just as exhaustive as the first.

With still no phone to be found, she came to a decision. She'd drive out to the eastern coast herself, to the work site. She'd surprise Rip. And if he was of the same mind, maybe they'd pass each other on the road first, like something out of a romantic comedy. And he'd flash his lights, because he'd see her first. They'd each pull over to their own side of the road. He'd jog across the street, risking his life and limb to hug her and apologize for the mix-up. They'd laugh.

They'd kiss...

A sharp knock startled Tatum from her reverie.

She'd been standing right there, at the door, ready to depart. Here it was. The funny, sweet, romantic mix-up. She swung the door open, all full of loving feelings and gooeyness inside the likes of which she was beginning to get used to.

"Why, *hello, you*," she purred as she batted her eyelashes and swung one hip out just so.

"Tatum."

It was Rip.

But he wasn't returning the flirtation.

His expression stony, his body tense. He didn't move to come in and sit down on the floor with the dogs. He didn't lean to kiss her. Was this it? Did he decide they definitely were *not* dating? That he didn't love and never could love her? Did he somehow find out she thought she might love him? Did her innermost feelings ruin *everything*?

"I tried to call."

"I'm sorry. I can't find my phone." She felt sheepish and ashamed. Usually, it didn't much bother Tatum that people couldn't reach her and got irritated when they couldn't. But now, she was the fool. Not the cell-phone addicts. It was Tatum. Tatum was the one who couldn't answer a simple phone call on a stupid cell phone. "I'm sorry," she said again, her voice cracking, like there might be other things she should be sorry for, too. She just didn't know what they were.

But his face broke. And in he stepped, finally lowering to one knee as Angus lumbered down the hall for his usual greeting. "Something happened at the site. I have to go back. I came here, because..." his voice trailed off and he looked up from Angus to Tatum. "Well, the police told me I needed to stick around."

"Police?" Tatum frowned deeply and lowered to pet Angus along with Rip. "What happened? Are you okay?"

His gaze was glassy, and he looked past her and into nothingness, scared or worried or—something worse. "We were excavating for the cafeteria. And one of the guys was down there, checking on something. He found..." the muscles in Rip's jaw clenched and slackened and clenched and slackened.

"What?" Tatum pressed. "What did he find?"

Rip licked his lips and ran a hand over his mouth before finally looking at Tatum. "He found *someone*."

CHAPTER 5—CADENCE

Cadence started that school day with urgency and passion. Her students felt it, she could tell. They were especially wide-eyed for a cold winter day.

She moved through her lessons with a fury and an intensity that maybe even frightened them a little, but no matter, *this* was what she had to do. She had to salvage the school. It was her newest compulsion. It could keep her distracted from her sleepless nights. It could be her new thing. And Cadence needed a new thing, oh did she.

First went Hendrik.

Then the girls—even Mila. Each one leaving her there, alone with their memories on the island.

Next was Tatum who somehow had managed to

pull off the opening of a business with relatively little assistance. Well, she *did* have assistance. Rip.

Lastly, the twins. Darla went back on her plan. She'd stay home. She didn't need Cadence to take care of them. Maybe Darla didn't even need Cadence to take care of her. Maybe she'd let Mason in eventually. Then, it'd just be Cadence. Cadence and who? Cadence and *what*?

Cadence finished one lesson and launched into the next, barely stopping for a breath until the lunch bell rang. It surprised her, the bell. Like she'd forgotten about taking any break, much less a full half-hour. Mondays, Mr. McGee covered lunch duty, which meant Cadence could stay in her room and eat in peace. Except, it didn't feel peaceful. She was uneasy and edgy.

Her packed lunch didn't do much to jostle her out of the odd buzz, either. Her phone sat in the top drawer of her desk, typically untouched until the end of the school day. But right now, Cadence had such an urge to talk to someone or see something or do something, she went for it.

With great surprise, Cadence saw she had nine missed calls and a string of thirteen unread text messages, from a couple of different sources, too.

All of the phone calls were from her sisters.

Darla and Tatum, both. But Cadence darted back into her messages to see what the emergency could be. She stood from her desk, both hands gripping her phone as she tapped away. In their sister group thread, it was a flurry of out-of-context blabber.

The first one was from Tatum. *Darla call me.*

Darla hadn't replied immediately, which Cadence took to mean she'd probably called. Then Tatum and Darla had returned to the thread. One after the other, interchangeably discussing the unknown drama and pressing Cadence to pick up her phone.

But if it *was* an emergency, a real emergency, they'd have called the school, and the secretary would have walked down to Cadence's classroom in person to deliver the urgent message. None of that happened, which meant Cadence was safe to assume it was a non-emergent matter or, worse, gossip.

Cadence moved to the next thread of messages. These were from just Darla, and entirely unrelated.

Any chance you can grab milk on your way home? If not, no problem!

Minutes later: *Never mind, sorry. I'll go tomorrow when I have the car.*

Another thread from Mila, who'd replied to

Cadence's message early that morning. *Thanks, Mom. Have a great day, too. I'm happy to know you're happy*

Sweetheart that she was. Sometimes, the girls called her Cadence. But when they called her Mom, it was everything. She smiled at the little note and, momentarily forgetting about whatever external thing was happening between Tatum and Darla, started to reply to Mila.

A phone call came through right then, interrupting her. She didn't recognize the number, and it looked to be a Detroit area code. Cadence was ready to mark it as spam, but something—maybe the buzz —stopped her. Instead, she answered the call.

"Is this Cadence Van Dam?"

"It is," she replied, trying to pin down the vaguely familiar voice.

"Hi, Cadence. This is Dr. Sanders." He cleared his throat. "*Kirk.*"

Her heart sank in her chest then rebounded up, bouncing into her throat and catching there. "Kirk?" she squeaked. She hadn't spoken to him since the animal shelter opening. Why was he calling now? She panicked and stalled. "Dr. Sanders, I mean." Maybe this was a professional call.

"Please," he replied right away, "call me Kirk." He sounded jovial about it and this made Cadence believe that no, it was not professional. It was personal.

"Right. *Kirk.*" Great name. An image of his face calibrated in her brain, and Cadence couldn't help but look forward to seeing him again soon. Hopefully outside of his in-home office.

"How are you? How were your holidays?" He was making small talk. Cadence marked this as a good sign.

She contemplated her answer briefly. To be thorough or not to be thorough, that was the question? She opted to go for it. "Great, thank you! I decided to return to the classroom full time. Last semester I was considering a family leave of absence, you know. Well, it's been a good decision. I'm here at school now." She was rambling, but she couldn't stop. "Darla and the boys are doing well. Tatum's shelter is up and running, and I think that's going well, too. Thanks to sponsorships like yours, not doubt." A little flattery never hurt anybody.

"I'm glad to hear that."

Cadence rushed to add, "And you? How were your holidays?"

"Relaxing! First time in years I haven't been running around shopping at the last minute." He chuckled, and Cadence decided she liked the sound of his chuckles.

She tried for a chuckle too, and though it was awkward, she felt they were flowing. She felt their conversation was coming easily, and she was happy to be talking to him. She needed a little stimulation, and maybe a casual friendship with Dr. Kirk Sanders could be that. Then again. He was her therapist. And, as if on cue, the conversation came to an uncomfortable silent pause. Cadence wanted to keep it going. To move past these niceties and invite him over for dinner with Darla and Tatum and her. Rip could come, too. An evening of adult engagement for all parties.

"Well," he said.

"Well," she said at the same time.

Again, they chuckled. Cadence started to say something more, something like, *do you have plans this coming Friday?*

But before either one of them could move the conversation along, another call beeped on Cadence's line. She glanced at the screen. Darla.

"Oh, um—"

"Right, I was actually calling, because—"

"Dr. Sanders? *Kirk*?" Cadence hated to get him off the line, but she really needed to field the family drama. Besides, she still didn't know *what* was going on with her sisters.

"Oh, yes?"

"I hate to do this, but I'm getting another call. Can I get back to you in, say, five minutes?"

"Sure. Sure!" he answered chirpily. "Talk soon."

She hung up and answered Darla. "What's going on?" Cadence all but snapped. It was hard to be sympathetic when Cadence was otherwise on a roll. And she hated to give into gossip, which she was *positive* this was about. Because, once again, if it were *actually* an emergency, her sisters would have gotten in touch through the school once they realized she didn't answer her cell during class.

"You answered!" Darla boomed over the line. "We've been calling you all morning."

"I know. I was teaching. What's going on? Are you okay? The boys? Tatum? What?"

"Yes, we're fine. Everyone is fine."

"Then what?" Cadence demanded. Lunch time was winding down. She had just minutes before students lined up in the hall. She still needed to call Kirk back. "What happened, Darla?"

"Okay, *so*—" Darla's tone gave it away. It *was*

gossip. Cadence wanted to hang up on her. She didn't, though, and instead listened on as Darla explained.

CHAPTER 6—DARLA

At last, Cadence answered her phone. Darla instantly launched into a recap of all the crazy events from that day.

"Okay, so, you know how Rip and his crew are building that new school on the eastern coast, right?"

"Of course." Of course, she did. If anyone was the most upset about the new school, it was Cadence.

Darla went on. "Well, they are a fair way through the project. You see, Rip had to put things on hold over Christmas break because the ground was *so* frozen. We had a few warm days, right? And they aren't doing that much in the way of digging or whatever, right?"

"Sure." Cadence was curt to the point of impatient, so Darla quickened her pace.

"Anyway, since there was a tiny bit of thaw—"

"The ground here doesn't thaw until May at the earliest, Darla," Cadence interrupted.

"Okay, well. I don't know. I guess it can be frozen and they can still dig? I don't know! Anyway, Cadence, Rip took his crew back out today to give it another go. They can't exactly do workarounds when it comes to the necessary excavations, but they have the right rig to make a go even if the ground is frozen." Darla was boring herself with all these technicalities, but they were *so, so, so* necessary. "Rip goes out there this morning, and they are working on the cafeteria, right?"

"Come on, Darla. Get to the point. I've got class starting soon."

"Sorry. Okay, so they've got the area prepped to dig for the footers, or whatever—I don't know how I even know this terminology. Anyway, Rip goes down there to the base of the rig before they start. Actually, wait. It might have been one of the crewmen?"

"Darla," Cadence barked.

"Sorry!" Darla knew she sounded like Tatum. Her excitement was overwhelming. A byproduct of being at home with two babies all day, maybe. "Well, *anyway*, something is sticking out of the ground."

"Sticking out? What, like, rebar?" Cadence said this with such scorn, that Darla was nearly giddy to drop the next bombshell.

"No. A *bone*."

At that, Cadence outright laughed. "A bone? Like, what? A dog bone?" She laughed again.

Darla kept her voice even and grave, though. "A *human* bone."

CHAPTER 7—TATUM

"What does this all mean?" Tatum asked Rip.

It was Monday late afternoon, and they'd gathered together at the boardwalk house, where Cadence was making supper. This, after a brief visit to the site. Cadence had wanted to see it for herself.

The police had questioned all of Rip's crew, or nearly all. They had told Rip to stay near, and that they'd be in touch.

Rip wasn't one to sit idly. So although Tatum and Darla were lounging on the sofa with the twins napping comfortably, he was setting the table and giving Cadence a hand. With little flourishes, he added a fork to each setting then answered Tatum. "I have no idea what it means, honestly."

Darla asked, "You've never dug up human remains on accident?"

Rip answered, "Nuh-uh. I mean, I've heard it happens, sure. Not to me, though."

Cadence chimed in from the stove, where she was grilling chicken breasts. "I heard it happened on the mainland. Just this past year!"

"Where? What?" Tatum couldn't imagine that there were bodies buried just beneath the very ground she walked on, either on Heirloom Island or in Birch Harbor. Though, to be fair, she didn't spend a lot of time in Birch Harbor. Still, even one body to have walked on—it gave her the shivers something bad. "In Birch Harbor?"

"No." Cadence left the kitchen and stood in the archway, facing the living room and the others. "It was out in the suburbs. A little town. Something hills."

"Harbor Hills. I know of it." Rip grabbed glasses from the bar and set about adding ice as he called over his shoulder. "I know a guy who has family up there."

"Who?" Tatum asked, finding herself jealous of the side of Rip's life that she didn't know about. She was being silly. Forcing herself to *not* care about what he said or did felt impossible though, and she couldn't stand not to get up and join him to hear his answer. "I'll get the wine out," she added casually, as if she didn't need to hang on his every word.

"Matt Fiorillo." Then he gave a jut of the chin to Darla. "Mason Acton—that's how I know Matt. Mason is, like, related to Matt's girlfriend's—I don't know. He's, like, related by marriage to Matt."

"Matt Fiorillo?" Cadence asked. She only knew of him because of the reunion they'd hosted the spring prior. Tatum remembered, because she remembered the Hannigan sisters. Now *that* was a crazy family. Tatum liked to know that hers wasn't the only one a little bit weird. There were others like them, too.

"There was a body found in Harbor Hills? By a contractor or something?" Darla asked. "What did it have to do with Matt Fiorillo?"

"Nothing that I know of. My point is simply that these things happen."

"Then why do the police want to question you?" Cadence asked him.

Tatum glared at her sister, but Cadence missed it, instead passing back to the stove to finish the chicken.

Rip, too, was unfazed. "We were the first to discover it. My guys were. I came down after. They always interview the person who finds human remains. Standard procedure."

"He can't go home until the police talk to him. Right Rip?" Tatum confirmed, a little excitement coursing through her veins.

"I guess. I mean, I'm sure I *could* go home, but it's the Island PD that's covering the case right now, and I might as well make things easy for them."

"You're not, like, a person of interest, though." Cadence said this without the perfunctory blasé that she ought to have. Instead, a twinge of suspicion colored her tone, and it bugged Tatum. A lot.

"He didn't bury the guy. Geez, Cade."

"So, it's a man?" Darla asked. She, too, had left the snoozing twins to join the conversation in the kitchen, proper. Plucking a raw carrot from the bag on the counter, she popped it into her mouth then helped with the salad. "The body they found was a man?"

"It wasn't a body," Rip corrected. "It was just a skeleton."

"A skeleton used to have a body. You say that like it's *less* than human." Cadence's attitude toward Rip was starting to push Tatum over the edge.

"What's wrong, Cadence?" Darla asked this, and then she exchanged a look with Tatum that proved it wasn't only Tatum who felt the tension mounting.

"Yeah," Tatum chimed in. "You're acting weird about it."

"I'm not acting weird. The whole situation is weird. That's all." Her voice deflated a little. "Anyway, I just think—it's a really big deal. To find human remains."

"Yeah," Tatum replied. "And where that school is going up? Kind of crazy." It's what Tatum didn't say that was important. That this could be perfect. Perfect for St. Mary's at least. Then again, not perfect for Rip. She frowned. "Rip, what does this mean for your project? Will you get back to work in a couple of days, or is this going to unrail things?"

Darla corrected her. "*De*-rail, Tatum."

Rip let out a sigh. "It means we're on hold until the police decide otherwise. It depends on a lot of factors. Who this person was, why they found themselves in a shallow grave on a lake island beach..." he trailed off.

"So he *was* a man?" Darla asked again.

Cadence gave a sigh of exasperation this time. "Darla, no one knows yet. Why does it even matter? Do you happen to know a guy who went missing or something?"

Darla seemed to consider this. "No. I guess not."

"Yeah, me either," Cadence replied, but even as she said it, her voice went hollow and tapered off into nothing. She returned to the chicken and removed them from the skillet. Tatum thought she looked a little shaken, then, but she wasn't sure why. Besides, Tatum knew how to cheer Cadence up.

"Anyway, is this *such* a bad thing?" she asked, elbowing her sister playfully.

Cadence looked at her as if she were a foreign object in a tranquil sea. Like Cadence didn't know what Tatum was doing there, in her kitchen, suddenly.

"What is it?" Tatum asked.

"What do you mean 'is this such a bad thing?' Finding human remains is never a good thing."

"Could be," Darla reasoned. "Maybe someone was looking for this person. Now, the search is over. The person has been found."

"Yeah, found *dead*," Cadence argued.

"Okay, fine. But you know what else this whole thing means? It means the new school is on hold. Yet *again*," Tatum pointed this out mischievously and in a silly way. But she was met with contemptuous looks from all three of the other adults.

Well, maybe not Rip. He gave her a discreet half smile.

But Cadence stole the moment back. "Tatum, that's incredibly insensitive."

Darla couldn't help but glob on, too. "And tacky." One of the boys started to fuss in the living room, and it broke things up until dinner.

Dinner. An awkward affair, all around. Made more awkward by the waiting game Rip was playing for the police. And even *more* awkward by Cadence's continued weird behavior about the body.

After they ate the chicken and a dessert of lemon meringue pie and after a round of coffees—and a hot cocoa for Darla—the four adults and two babies settled into the living room. It was past seven now, and Rip was beginning to wonder aloud if the police were going to contact him at all.

"How are they going to get in touch?" Tatum wondered aloud.

Rip shrugged. Darla yawned. Cadence shifted on the armchair.

Rip took the hints. "You know what? They can get in touch with me back on the mainland. I don't need to keep you ladies up. You must all be tired. You have to work tomorrow. And the babies." Rip gave a soft smile to the boys who cooed happily in their playpen. They didn't mind staring up at flashing doodads. Babies were easily entertained like that, Tatum realized.

"You're not keeping me up," Tatum protested. "I stay up late."

Rip squeezed the top of her thigh. The sensation rippled like an echo throughout her body and Tatum ignored the fact that her sisters, unlike Tatum, did *not* protest.

In fact, Cadence had an idea. "If you feel like you need to stay on the island, you're welcome to sleep here."

Tatum shot her a look. *What*?

"Here?" she asked, trying for some degree of clarification. "Where, though?"

"You're not sleeping here. You've been at the shelter every night for over a week. Maybe even two weeks. Or longer."

"I was going to stay here tonight, though."

"What about the animals?" Darla asked. And Darla was right. Tatum wasn't actually going to stay at the boardwalk. She needed to let her dogs out. And she needed to check on the tenants, as she called the shelter pets.

"Well, it's getting late. I wasn't sure I wanted to drive back down the island in the dark." This was a complete fabrication. Tatum did what she wanted, when she wanted. And sometimes, safety be darned.

Darla, judgmental Darla, lifted a knowing eyebrow at her. "Well, if you were going to stay here because it's too dark to drive, then maybe Rip could go to the shelter. He can let the dogs out, right Rip?" She looked at him and Rip looked at Tatum.

It was Cadence, though, who dragged the elephant into the center of the room and propped him on the ottoman. "Rip, it's not a bad idea if you stay local. Tatum, you need to take care of the pets. If you're not comfortable driving home, why not take Rip with you?"

Tatum felt like a giddy schoolgirl. Her sister was flat-out giving her permission to take a man home. A man who had taken Tatum to dinner precisely four times. A man who came by with coffee over five times and who texted her morning and night. Whose lips she'd kissed and arms she'd felt around her. A man who Tatum didn't quite have a name for, other than Rip Van Dam. Other than her sister's brother-in-law. This man, who was probably the first man in Tatum's whole life to grab her attention so exclusively and keep it there...this handsome, funny, kind man...

"To spend the night?" Tatum blurted out.

Cadence and Darla glanced at one another. Cadence lowered her voice. "You're an adult, Tatum."

But Darla, prim and proper and uptight Darla, wouldn't give her stamp of approval. She set her jaw and reached down for one of the boys. "I'm going to bed. Whatever you two choose to do, just...*be safe.*" Darla said this with such a sour tone that Tatum second guessed her interest in letting Rip come stay at The Manger House with her.

Rip, however, didn't seem to notice or mind. He sprang up. "I'm sure I could go home, but the local PD didn't ask for my phone number. Cadence, if they come by, will you let them know where I am? I think it's most convenient for them if I'm around tonight and tomorrow morning. A boat trip out to Birch Harbor would drag things out unnecessarily. And I'm sure they have a lot of questions for me."

"Okay," Tatum replied, her voice full of hope. "It's settled then. We'll stay at The Manger House together."

"Great," Rip answered. They both stood and hesitated for a moment, Cadence's and Darla's eyes fixed on them. A cloud of expectancy hung in the air.

"Should we...go?" Tatum asked everyone, rather than just Rip.

"Yeah." He pushed his hands down into his pockets and made a shallow bow in the direction of Cadence. "Thank you so much for having me to dinner, Cadence. We'll have to do this again. Next time, I'll host."

"Rip?" Cadence asked impishly. "Just go."

Tatum reached for his hand, and they started for the door, but just as Rip turned the knob to open it, a knock came on the other side.

CHAPTER 8—CADENCE

Cadence had no choice but to let Rip and Tatum back into the house along with two detectives. She first shooed Darla and the babies upstairs for bed, then put on a fresh pot of coffee while her newest guests situated themselves around the dining room table.

"So," Cadence began, serving a mug to each person. "Has there been any identification made?"

The older detective answered. "No, ma'am. We're waiting on results from dental records. It's all we have to go on right now."

"Do you know if it's a man? A woman?" she asked.

"We're not releasing any further information to the public quite yet."

"I'm hardly the public. You're here to interview my brother. It's a family matter, no?"

The man gave her a look, and Rip cleared his throat. Cadence realized that she was wrong, and it wasn't her business. Not yet, at least.

"Right. Right!" she said brightly before pushing up from the table. "I'll be in the kitchen." Cadence looked at Tatum. "Dishes, Tate?"

"Oh! Yes. Dishes."

The two sisters left Rip to be questioned and scurried around the breakfast bar and into the kitchen, a relatively modest distance from the police and Rip but removed enough to offer privacy.

"This is sort of exciting," Tatum whispered as they set about soaking a tower of plates. "Right?"

"How is this exciting? It's stressful. For Rip, first of all. And, really, I mean, Tatum, it's dark. I think it's just really dark." Cadence stole the moment to cross herself and send up a prayer. It was dark. But—well—it was also a little timely, maybe.

Please, God, let this work out for the best. For everyone, but...if this is meant to help St. Mary's. Let it. Please, God.

She cringed at herself for thinking as much and returned, mentally, to the position that it was dark.

Not timely. Just dark. Another prayer crossed over her heart and up out her soundless lips.

God, I leave it to Your will. Amen.

Tatum's voice hadn't lost its thrill. "Well, it's a skeleton, though, Cadence. It could be ancient. You know the Huron people lived in this area. Some evidence has even said there was once a civilization on Heirloom Island."

"That's not true. It's a myth. The Huron were never stupid enough to set up camp in the middle of a freezing-cold lake." Cadence shivered at the thought. An ancient native burial ground? "There's no way that's what this is. And anyway, they only found one skeleton. If anything, it was a monk from that old monastery."

"Old monastery?" Tatum scrubbed. Then, thoughtfully, she asked, "Well, anyway, I can't believe you're not happier about it, though. Be real, Cadence. This means the charter school is stalled even further. Who knows—maybe they won't be able to open for the new school year. You were so worried about that. This discovery absolutely bene-fits you."

"The death of a human being benefits no one, unless that human being was evil or something. And even then, I don't wish death on people, Tatum. You shouldn't either." She hated sounding like a mom, and it wasn't as though Tatum was missing a moral compass. But Tatum should bite her tongue. She was being callous, at the minimum. Cruel, even.

"I don't!" Tatum's soapy hands flew up. "I didn't kill this person and I absolutely do not wish death on anyone—good or bad. I even question capital punishment."

"Of course you do," Cadence murmured cynically. And Tatum wasn't lying, Cadence knew. She was a bit of a bleeding heart, and not only when it came to animals. Tatum was the type to open her house to anyone, not only the forlorn furballs that she already did. That absolute sympathy then, also meant she felt for Cadence too. And for St. Mary's and the children who went there. "You know, the new charter school isn't all bad. It could drive more families to move here."

"It's not good for St. Mary's. I know that, Cade. If a new school opens, you'll lose the kids who come to your school by default. Not the Milas of the world—you already lost those ones. I'm talking about the precious remaining few who aren't willing to board a ferry in the dead of January to cross a partially frozen lake. The ones unwilling to stay home and do schoolwork when the lake is entirely frozen. The ones stuck here."

"The kids who come to St. Mary's now aren't just stuck with us. They want to be there. Lots of them do." Cadence knew this was an exaggeration. She knew she had a lot more praying to do. Praying that St. Mary's would withstand the excitement of the new school. Praying that somehow the new school wouldn't affect their beautiful little Catholic school.

Tatum fell silent for a moment. Cadence glanced through to the dining room. Rip was gesturing with his hands, his voice clear. She turned the faucet off and motioned for Tatum to stay quiet.

Now they could both hear Rip clearly as he carried on explaining everything he could possibly share about the discovery.

Mid-sentence, he went on, "—and I told the guys to back off and get out of there. I'm not a total dolt, so I kept the space clear as I could. We'd already done enough damage. Who knew if we'd disrupted the scene? Not sure if it was officially going to become a crime scene, but you know, I wanted to play it safe."

The detective asked, "Before you broke ground on the project, had you noticed anything unusual in the area? Say, a crude tombstone, scraps of clothing —anything that might have preempted this find?"

There was a brief pause before Rip replied. "Not on land. The site itself is inland some ways, as you know. Not safe to build too close to the lake when it's a school building we're talking about. Anyway, not every last kid can swim. The folks from the school emphasized they wanted ample distance from the water, but a good view of it, too."

"They were concerned about the water as a safety hazard," the detective replied.

"Yes."

"But they commissioned the build for a distance of no less than half a mile out from the lake's edge."

"Right, well, there was a building there previously, and in order to save money, the school folks wanted us to make use of the main pad, utilities, all that."

The detective jumped on this. "There was a building there previously—right. The old monastery?" He quieted for a beat then said, "But that's been gone for many, many years."

"I don't know much about that." Rip remained calm and cooperative. Cadence was impressed. She'd buckle under such heat, and not because of any measure of guilt but because of the presumption of guilt in these matters. Everyone was a suspect, even innocents.

"Yeah, that monastery. You just mentioned it?" Tatum whispered. "So, it's true?"

Cadence nodded. "I've heard about it at school. I think it was Franciscan?" She gave her head a shake. "When Heirloom Island was first settled, there was a whole legion of Catholics. They started on Birch Harbor, but the founding family got into a feud with another settling family or something. The group split and since it was harder to get to the island, the ones who lived on Heirloom thought they'd attract people by really building out the church community here."

"You know a lot about this."

"It's a big part of the parish's tradition, and the school's, too. Anyway, back then, priests weren't as hard to come by. A strong monastery was basically an assurance that people could come to Heirloom, not only to live but to visit, too. And we'd have a steady supply of priests both for St. Mary's and the mainland parishes. It was a win-win."

"What happened to it?"

"It closed a while back. A good fifteen years, or something."

"Why? Because of scandals in the Church?"

Cadence should bite her lip. To spill such gossip was unchristian, but then, Tatum was her sister. Was it really gossip if you were just bringing your own sister up to speed? "Not the scandals in the Catholic Church, no."

Tatum looked at her expectantly. "Okay?"

"There was one scandal at the monastery. But that's unverified. It's just talk. Rumor. One of the monks went back on his vows. It brought a lot of shame to the parish as well as the monastery, and they were already teetering on the balance of low membership and interest. So, it folded."

"What vow did he break?"

"Again, this is hearsay, Tate. It could be made up for all I know."

"Usually," Tatum replied, "every seed of truth carries a rumor."

Despite the serious, earnest look on her sister's face, Cadence couldn't help but laugh. "The saying is that every rumor carries a seed of truth. You got it a little backwards."

Tatum waved her off. "Well? What was it? What vow did he break?"

"The vow of chastity. That's the rumor at least." Cadence hadn't really concerned herself with the monk who'd taken a lover. It was neither here nor there, especially now, so long after.

Tatum, however, was scandalized. Her mouth fell wide open and her eyes doubled. "He had an affair!? Get out of here." Her gasp came after, as she processed it. "With who?"

"No one knows. It all goes back to rumor. Some said she was a wayward widow. Others claim she was a local divorcee with a penchant for adventure." Cadence chuckled. "That's where the lore falls apart."

"Did anyone know them? Or see them? Like, what happened afterwards?"

"They skedaddled, I guess. I don't really know. It's not part of the story, which again makes it all the more suspect to begin with. If it had really happened, there'd have been fallout. The shamed monk would've fallen off the radar, sure. But what about the woman? She'd probably be around to tell her tale."

CHAPTER 9

Her family was growing. Adding stress to a marriage already as thin as the last bit of lake ice. The bit that had managed to last through the winter, but it was almost summer now, and the air warmed by degrees every day. The ice was brittle and muddy and fragile like bone China.

They turned to a counselor, the family did. On her behalf more than on the marriage's behalf. It was an older woman with strong ties to the church, the deacon's wife, actually. She ran her own in-home therapy practice on the northeast shore of the island, and it was there that the troubled husband and wife found themselves on one brilliant Sunday morning.

The woman—Dr. Sanders was her name—had

recommended a retreat put on by the monastery. What the couple didn't know was that this was a last-ditch effort to retreat to save the final vestiges of what was once the island's thriving religious community.

They showed up together, but not hand-in-hand, at the doorstep of a teetering building—poorly made, no doubt—to be met with men in brown robes who looked otherwise like regular people. Not like the bald-headed monks from movies.

They were led to a barren backroom where one particular man stood in prayer, facing a row of prayer candles. Incense smoke billowed about him and when he turned, she was taken aback. This was no monk like any she'd seen—real or movie. He was even more regular than the ones who'd guided them in there. Tall and slender, but not thin. A full head of hair. Strong jaw and a prominent Adam's apple and all the makings of a normal, handsome person dressed in a frumpy, scratchy-looking brown robe with a rope tied around his trim waist.

"Welcome to the Holy Isle Monastery. We're here to pray with you and to help you."

"Good to meet you," her husband grunted. It came out false and insincere, and she didn't care.

The monk's eyes lingered on her a moment too

long. When his heavy gaze moved away, she felt thirsty and desperate for it to return. Her husband's presence melted into irrelevance and an unruly, indecent want welled up deep inside of her.

They started with a group prayer, each lowered onto a hard wooden chair, heads solemnly ducked, and eyes closed. Hers fluttered open every two seconds, the consequence of insecurity and wonton need, to be sure.

The prayer ended and three sets of eyes rose up, a little sheepish and awkward at such an intimate start to an intimate thing in an intimate place like this wooden-walled room with its candles and its incense. "Now, what brings you to the Holy Isle?"

Her husband snorted, "Our marital therapist said this was a couples' retreat."

She remained silent; her stare remained fixed. On the strange religious man.

"Yes. You're in the right place. I suppose what I'm asking is, what sequence of events saw you end up here as opposed to, say, dinner on the mainland and a movie after."

Another snort. "We eat dinner. We watch movies."

"Is your marriage failing?" Spoken so bluntly, the

words hit like a series of perfectly aimed arrows. Not to her heart, though. To her husband's.

He threw up his hands. "I've tried everything." He hooked a thumb at her. "She wants out. We have children."

"Is it that your children are keeping you together, then?"

She frowned. "We took vows."

The stranger leaned away, his light eyes holding her gaze yet. "Vows." He seemed to roll another thought around in his mind and then his mouth—or was that his tongue she saw? She pursed her lips.

"Marriage is a sacrament," he added. "Just like Baptism, Confirmation, Eucharist, Reconciliation, Anointing of the Sick, and Holy Orders." The final two words seem to cling to the warm, woodsy air, vibrating through her. She'd never do something so extreme. Becoming a nun was for those who had nothing else. But then, if that were true, why was she sitting in front of a perfectly handsome monk, who might become a perfectly virtuous priest under the perfectly Catholic sacrament of Holy Orders?

And was it just the Holy Orders that were so extreme? Or were all seven sacraments so dangerous?

This thought bore further consideration.

"Vows are a serious thing, and one that many people take too lightly." The monk's voice turned firm.

The husband and wife exchanged a look. It was the first time they'd shared a common thought, or, at least, the first time it was readily apparent that they'd shared a common thought.

"Children, vows," the husband said. Then, "And love. I love her from the depths of my soul. I always will."

"And do you love him?" the monk asked her flatly.

She set her jaw. The answer was simple, actually. Complicated and simple. She looked at her husband then crossed her arms over her chest before returning to look at the monk. "Yes."

CHAPTER 10—CADENCE

As she dried the cast iron pan with a dishtowel, Tatum returned their conversation to the investigation and the site of the remains. "So it was a monastery? That's what those old ruins are? Where the new school is going? Ruins from an old monastery? How come the monastery crumbled away like that? It's not like it was centuries old."

"Not long after it closed, a bad storm hit the lake. It wiped out most of the residences on the eastern coast. I'm sure it pulled most of the monastery down. The building was simple, austere. And, it actually was old. Very old. Not centuries, but close to one century."

"Was it closer to the water?"

"Maybe." Cadence finished drying the last of the

plates as she watched the detectives stand to go. "But the end of the monastery was the beginning of the end of St. Mary's, too. Without that sort of draw, and of course with the news of the scandals inside of the church, membership slowly dwindled. It's now nearly dried up. Over half of our students aren't Catholic. A quarter aren't even religious or spiritual."

"I'm not religious," Tatum pointed out. "But I'm spiritual."

"And that's okay, Tate," Cadence replied, looking at her sister earnestly. "Plus, I don't think it's bad that our students come from non-religious families, because our mission as a school isn't to convert anyone. It's to share God's word, yes. And even more than that, it's to set an example of a Christ-like life. We exist to nurture the family—the church family and the individual families of our parish and student base."

Rip returned from seeing the detectives out. He rubbed his hands together. "Welp, guess that's over with."

Cadence smiled at him. "Did they say when you can start back on your construction?"

"I'm not sure." He looked uneasy. "It'll depend on who the remains belonged to, and—"

"And what?" Tatum asked excitedly. Cadence held her breath, not because she wanted the project to fall apart or be stalled, but because...well, because it was quite the small-town news.

Rip gave them each a grave look. "If there are more remains."

CHAPTER 11—CADENCE

The next day, St. Mary's was abuzz with the gossip of the unfolding events. Mr. McGee called a morning staff meeting. They began with a prayer for the soul of the person found. After that, he lectured the group.

"This matter has nothing to do with St. Mary's. I feel that we must be staunch in our refusal to engage in gossip about who the deceased might be and what might have happened. Any such talk is mere conjecture—to use a judicial term—and as such, qualifies as nothing short of tale telling. Frankly, it's a bad example, and I won't tolerate it."

Cadence agreed with him, fundamentally, but she couldn't help but feel curious. And anyway, the whole mess might well and truly affect the progress of the new school build. That *did* concern St. Mary's. It'd affect their staffing and enrollment, potentially. Shouldn't they reach out to the new administration? Cadence felt it important to ask Mr. McGee, and so she did. "Mr. McGee, would it not be prudent to contact Mr. Rutherford and his team to see what their plans are?"

"It's early for that, Ms. Van Dam." He appeared a bit ruffled to be challenged, and the sudden hushing of the staff's whispers contributed to a blanket of palpable anticipation.

"With all due respect, Mr. McGee, is it ever too early for a kind remark or a gesture of support? Regardless of our conflict of interest with Mr. Rutherford and the new school, the Christian thing to do is to offer a helping hand." Cadence didn't mean to sound high and mighty, but she realized she definitely sounded that way, and Mr. McGee's stricken expression confirmed that her tone was smug and haughty. So, she quickly added, "I'm sorry. I don't mean to suggest we aren't acting as Christians now. I just mean that perhaps the right thing to do isn't to mind our own business."

Mr. McGee adjusted his glasses. "Very well, I can agree with that, Ms. Van Dam. Perhaps you'd be willing to take on the role of ambassador?"

Cadence's heart stopped for a beat before starting up in a harder pounding. She'd never been a leader at the school. Not back when she was full of the vim and vigor of her early teaching years and not now. But there was something deep inside of her, living in her, like a mystery of faith, that told her she was to spearhead this thing, whatever it became. Whether it was a contract of friendship or a chance to learn the truth about the human remains or even, maybe, an opportunity to save the one thing she had left in this world, her school. Whatever it was, she was to say yes. "Okay," Cadence replied. "I can do that."

That Tuesday was crazy. Everyone had an opinion about what Cadence should say to Mr. Rutherford, and none of their opinions jived with her overall goal: to offer an olive branch.

Come lunch time, she settled down at her desk and collected her thoughts as her phone sat squarely on her desk, between her hands which acted like frames around the device.

Something was bothering her, like a little niggling worm in her brain, pushing through, trying to be remembered. What was it? A sense of deja vu wasn't helping, and so Cadence flipped over the scrap of paper upon which was Mr. Rutherford's phone number.

Instead, she tapped her text message app.

Recent texts didn't shake loose that little worm.

She frowned at her classroom, the empty chairs. The blackboard—a relic of days gone long by. Still nothing.

Cadence returned to her phone and tapped open the phone call history. Maybe Darla would remember what it was Cadence couldn't pin a finger to. She scrolled to Darla's last call, and that's when she saw it. Saw *him*.

Of course.

Dr. Sanders.

Kirk.

Cadence's breath caught in her throat. It was such an odd feeling, this. And being now busier than ever and having more clarity than ever, she was fairly certain she could nail down exactly why her breath caught in her throat when she saw that man's name. Why her stomach lifted up as if it was suspended in her belly, a phantasmic organ.

Therapy. Cadence didn't need therapy anymore. What she felt when she saw Dr. Sanders' name was elation at a self-revelation. Elation at the recognition that Cadence was, by and large, doing well for herself. She didn't need a shrink to ask her how she felt about that. It was easy to know that Cadence felt good about feeling good.

But then, if that was true, why had this business with the human remains kept her awake at night? Why was she unreasonably irritated with Tatum for being so flippant about the whole thing? Why was Cadence encouraging Tatum to go out with Rip Van Dam, of all people!

Cadence was not herself, no. But she was happy. Right? That was possible, right? To not be oneself but still be happy?

She tapped Kirk's name.

CHAPTER 12—DARLA

Day two of being a stay-at-home mom, and Darla still felt nothing but bliss. Until she realized she really *did* need to go out for milk. And not only that, but diaper wipes were running low. And it'd been a while since she'd had a pot of night cream to slather on her face.

So, she decided to brave the cold and bundle the boys in their carriers and herself in one of Cadence's fur-lined down jackets before calling Tatum to come back to the boardwalk house and give her a lift to the market.

Tatum, who'd had to say a reluctant goodbye to Rip the night prior, came almost immediately.

She looked bedraggled, too. Her hair pushed back into a loose-fitting beanie that slumped on top, and her face devoid of anything short of a layer of sunscreen, visible by its white globs not well rubbed in, Tatum was hardly looking herself.

"What's wrong with you?" Darla asked, as they loaded the babies into the back seat of Tatum's truck.

"Nothing."

Tatum fell quiet again, but once they got driving, Darla thought up questions that might spark greater responses.

"How are the intakes? You've got two dogs right now, right?"

Tatum took in a breath and let it out, and her shoulders visibly relaxed. "Yes. They're good. I think I might have found a home for one. I'm putting them both onto the website this week. It's ready now, so that's good."

"How are the sponsorships coming along?" Darla knew that Tatum relied on grants and other free money to keep the mortgage payments coming in and the utilities turned on. Not to mention basics like pet food, collars, leashes, beds, cleaning supplies...and then of course money for herself to live on, which was the goal. Tatum wanted nothing more than to sustain herself there at The Manger House, without help from her sisters.

But it was a stretch. Just as it would soon become

a stretch for Darla to simply...stay home. For now, though, she had a little cash from her last paycheck and Cadence was generous enough to grant an allowance on top of that.

"And Rip?" Darla asked. She was far more curious about why Rip didn't stay the night with Tatum after all. "He didn't stay over?"

"No." An angry red colored Tatum's washed-out white cheeks. "He didn't. You don't have to worry. Everyone's dignity is preserved and intact."

Darla gave her a look before glancing back at the boys. They were way too little to appreciate the tenor of the conversation, but Darla wasn't about to take a chance. She lowered her voice. "I didn't mean sleep over as in sleep *with*. I just meant—well...What's going on with you two, anyway?"

At this, Tatum's face drained of its color. Her hands relaxed on the steering wheel and she looked all of fifteen years old. "I don't know. It's like we're dating, but we're not together or something. We don't...talk about it. You know?"

"You're not *official*. I get it." Darla thought about the boys' dad, Hunter, and the early days of their relationship. It was all very regimented from the get go. Three days to boyfriend-girlfriend. Six months to *I love you*. One year to engagement. And it would have been one more year to marriage. They fell short of that timeline when they'd eloped at eleven months, though.

Tatum pulled her beanie from her head, and her staticky hair feathered up, making her look even younger. "It's not about sleeping together or labels, even. I mean—we're *so* not there yet. I'm not like that." She stole a look at her sister, but Darla was working hard to remain impassive and free from judgment. Her sister needed her to be objective and reasonable but also, mostly, compassionate.

"What's it about?" Darla asked mildly.

Tatum had pulled the truck into the parking lot of the Bait Shop, parking up front so they didn't have a long ways to haul the baby carriers. She looked thoughtful for a moment. "It's about the fact that he brings me coffee?" She asked it more than stated it. "And that he kisses me on the cheek, and then, when he kisses me on the lips I'm waiting for more, and it doesn't come."

Darla kept still and quiet.

"And it's about the fact that Angus loves him, and all the others do, too. And how he took one of my first kittens to come to the shelter. It's about how he makes me laugh, and it's just so freaking easy, Darla.

Being with him is so easy." She shook her head. "It sucks."

At that, Darla blurted out a laugh. "Sucks? It sounds the exact opposite of sucky. It sounds—" Darla searched for the right word, "*perfect.*"

"Perfect would mean I'd know what we were doing and where we were going," Tatum replied.

"And this coming from the least organized, most carefree, spontaneous person I have ever met in my life." Darla snorted. "Since when do you want to know what you are doing and where you are going?"

Tatum seemed to think it over. "Since I moved here and opened the shelter and things that I had always sort of kind of really, really wanted to do started happening. Since, like, my dreams came true." She looked at Darla. "Since I met Rip."

CHAPTER 13—TATUM

Unsatisfied in her conversation with her sister, Tatum decided to stop talking about romance with Darla. Darla proved to be no assurance that Rip liked Tatum, and that's what Tatum was hoping to achieve. A sense of direction. An outsider's observation on what he thought of her. Of course, Tatum knew that the shortest point between two distances was a straight line. She *should* ask Rip flat out what he felt for her. But that felt like something reserved for normal people, and Tatum knew she wasn't exactly normal. For starters, she didn't even believe in romance. She had no interest in a love story. All she wanted was her animals and to save more of them. So Rip was nothing short of a fastball—or whatever the saying was.

Darla grabbed a shopping cart. "Meet you at the front?"

"I'll just come with you," Tatum replied, taking the cart from her sister to push it. "I don't need much."

They shopped. Darla fretted over whether to get generic this or brand-name that. Tatum stayed quietly thoughtful, her brain fixed on the silly question of whether a man returned her feelings for him. The impressive thing, though, was the fact that Tatum had feelings for a man to begin with. Maybe she didn't. Maybe it was...something else. Maybe she liked Rip a lot as a friend.

Then again, if that were the case, why would she notice little things about him. Like how when he pushed up his sleeves, she could see muscles rippling beneath his tanned skin? And how his Adam's apple bobbed when he drank, and it reminded her of a Gatorade commercial? And his hair—one time he showed up at her place and it had gotten wet from the snow or something, but all she could picture was Rip emerging from a fresh, hot shower, his curls wet against his forehead and smelling like soap and—

"What do you think?" Darla's voice dissolved the daydream.

Tatum turned her attention to two jars, Darla held one in each hand. Organic night cream with ceramides. Darla twisted it for Tatum to see the back label. "It's got retinol."

"Okay?"

"Or this." Darla made a face and showed her the second jar more closely. It was Mega Mart's version of something similar to the organic one. Night cream for smoothing skin and diminishing fine lines.

Tatum squinted at Darla's face. "Your face looks fine. You don't need either one."

"I do need night cream, yes. And, by the way, you do, too. Everyone should put cream on at night and sunscreen in the morning. But I have half a bottle of sunscreen. I just need the night cream."

Tatum was immediately bored by this, but even so, she ran a hand up her cheek. It did feel a little dry, as far as face skin could go. "I have lotion at home somewhere."

Darla gave her a look then returned to the jars. "I really need the retinol, though."

"Well, how much is it?" A simple enough question to help them discern the best choice.

"It's twenty dollars."

If Tatum had been sipping on a coffee, she'd

choke it up. "Twenty dollars! For *that*?" The jar was miniature. It'd last a week at best. "Twenty dollars!"

Darla read her mind. "It lasts a month!"

"How? Do you only use it for one application in a month?"

"You use a tiny bit, Tatum!" There was no humor in either's voice. They were basically arguing, there, in The Bait Shop. The most mundane of arguments, too. An argument about spending money. And they weren't even married.

Tatum just sighed. "It's your money. Get it if you want."

"I *do* want it. But it's not my money to spend."

"What do you mean?" Tatum asked.

"It's our money. I mean, we're all sharing right now. I can't just spend twenty dollars on night cream."

"Then why are you considering it?"

Darla looked like she might cry. "Because I usually get this one."

"It's okay to be on a budget, Darla." Tatum said this as softly as possible. She rested a hand on her sister's shoulder. It had to be hard being a new mom and not working. Especially for Darla. Her whole world was upended. More than Tatum's to be sure. "Forget the cream. We can make some. I've made lotion and soaps before. It's fun. *And*—" she poked Darla in the cheek and twisted her finger for extra teasing. "Organic."

Darla's eyes cleared of budding tears and she smiled. "I love you."

"I love you, too."

"But Tatum—" Darla frowned again "—I have to make some money." Darla reshelved the cream, duly defeated by the matter. Tatum pushed the cart on, sad for her sister now.

The best thing to do next was problem solve. "Well, if you want to be home with the boys *and* make money, then you just have to find a remote position. They're all the rage now, right? Everyone's working from home these days. Have you looked for jobs online?"

"I looked at the college to see if they were holding any online seminars or asynchronous courses."

"I don't know what a-sink-whatever means, but are they? Holding any, I mean?"

Darla shook her head. "I don't know what else I could do. I'm not qualified for anything other than teaching or drama. Some literature, obviously."

"What if you wrote a book and tried to sell it online?"

Darla laughed. "No. Way too much work. I don't know the first thing about writing a book. And what if no one wants to buy it? Then I've wasted hundreds of hours. Maybe thousands."

Tatum held up her hands in surrender. "Okay, okay. But just because you have a degree in teaching theater doesn't mean you can't do something else. There's plenty of online work. What about entering data? Isn't that a thing?"

"Data entry. Yeah. It is. I'd probably have to train."

"Well, that's okay. You train for it, then you get a job. And you make money from home. Voila!" Satisfied she'd solved the problem, Tatum smiled and pushed the cart on.

"Actually, what I was thinking was that we could maybe amp up the events thing Cadence has started. She hasn't done much with it, but we could really make something of that. I could take over, maybe."

Tatum looked curiously at Darla. "Rent out the house for events again?"

"Yeah. Right?"

"But, isn't the issue that Cadence is having a hard time making a go of it over the winter?"

"Well, sure, but we don't have to host winter

events. We can focus on the warmer months. Make all of our money there, you know?"

Tatum nodded. "And I'm sure Cadence would split it fifty-fifty with you." Tatum meant this earnestly, but Darla's face broke and she started to cry for real this time.

"Darla, what is it?"

They shuffled to the corner of the dairy refrigerators, out of view of any other shoppers. Tatum stood in front of Darla to block her upsetness from others and to block others from the scene, too. "What?" She pulled her sister's hands from her face, but it was too late. Darla was full-blown crying, and the tears were starting to plunk down on the boys' little squished faces.

Despite her state, though, Darla wiped the salty wetness from them and cooed at them to assure them that their mother was okay. They were okay. Safe. They were all okay. Through one last sob, though, Darla replied, "I can't just take on Cadence's extra income. She's given us so much. Your down payment. A home. Two homes, for goodness' sake." She wiped another tear. "You know, Tate?"

"I know. But we're all here together. We're in it together."

"But we can't just depend on each other like this

for everything for the rest of our lives. We each deserve independence. And, Tatum, Cadence needs it the most."

"What do you mean?"

"Don't you see? She's too wrapped up in helping other people. Her whole world is about taking care of us. Right now. And before us? It was taking care of Mila and Faye and Lotte. And before them?"

Tatum shrugged, helplessly confused.

"Hendrik." Darla swallowed and it looked like her crying was over for good. "Tatum, Cadence married this guy who took care of her, right? She got so used to that. But what they had was more than an arrangement like we kind of thought."

"I never thought it was an arrangement," Tatum protested. "I always thought they were in love."

"Well, you were right then. They were. They loved each other more than two people can. Cadence can't move on. But when he got sick, things got bad between them."

"Bad? How?"

"Hendrik relied one hundred percent on Cadence. She became like his mother. She did everything for him. She felt like in order to deserve his love, she had to go above and beyond." Darla knitted her eyebrows for a moment and seemed to think. Then, she looked past Tatum and to the rest of the store before dropping her voice. "I always thought she was, like, scared of something."

"Scared?" Tatum was confused. "Scared of what? Hendrik?"

"No. No, not of Hendrik. She wasn't afraid of him. She was afraid of losing him."

"Losing him to what? Cadence was perfect. She is perfect." Tatum shook her head. "Hendrik adored her, I always thought."

"I think it had less to do with Hendrik and more to do with the mystery behind his ex."

Tatum nodded slowly, processing what she knew. "You mean Katarina."

Darla grimaced and took the cart from Tatum to press on and finish their shopping excursion. "You'd be, too, right?"

"Afraid of Katarina? But how? She's gone."

Darla replied ominously. "I think Cadence is afraid she'll come back."

CHAPTER 14

The marital retreat carried on every Saturday for seven successive Saturdays, come rain or shine. With every single one, the curriculum was scripted and tight, and the monk, whom they just called Brother, was serious and unwavering in his fidelity to the program.

The second Saturday they went, the baby was especially fussy, and the usual babysitter was unavailable. This meant they'd bring the children to the retreat with them or have to skip. Skipping, apparently, was not an option.

So, the family stuffed themselves in the SUV and made their way to the eastern coast of the island, pleading for forgiveness and asking if there happened to be a rec room or something where the kids could safely play.

The husband was wholly uncomfortable with it all. With leaving the kids in another room, with having to bring them, and with the retreat. She wasn't too worried about the kids. The oldest was old enough to call 9-1-1 or report any funny business. It was the retreat, though, that bothered her. The being there together, as a family. So confined in an odd, old monastery at the lip of Lake Huron. It made her feel trapped. Even more trapped than in their house, which also sat on the lake and was degrees smaller than the monastery.

Now, if she were just trapped with Brother—oh, how she hated calling him *Brother*—that would be another matter. She figured that if this were individual therapy, she might really get something out of it. She might find out why she wasn't all keen on being married or having children or the whole wife-and-mother charade.

Okay, charade was a harsh word. She was doing it. Living it. Being the wife and being the mother. But then these glimpses came to her. Glimpses of what could have been.

"Well, are they?" The question stirred her from her inner thoughts. The couple was sitting uncomfortably in the wooden chairs across from Brother. The husband's mind was probably back with the children in the other room. Her mind was miles away.

"Are they?" she repeated. Her husband nudged her with his elbow. "Baptized. The kids." He was annoyed. "The baby isn't." Then he gave her a sharp look.

But she didn't care. Not at all. Not even enough to offer a shrug.

Brother cared. "Would you like to talk about this privately with me?" he asked her.

She snapped to. The hope of a thrill waking her up. "Yes."

The husband left as begrudgingly as she'd come there. He took the children and agreed to come back in an hour. He agreed that the wife needed a deeper session. He *agreed* to it all.

And then it was just the two of them.

The monk. And the wife.

"What does baptism mean to you?" Brother asked once they were all alone.

She peered at him curiously. "What does it mean to you?"

He blushed. "It means the beginning. A fresh start. And it means a promise."

"But babies can't make promises."

"Their parents can. And do."

"What if the baby has no parents?"

"Then it's upon the church to step in."

She thought about this. "How?"

"Different ways. Oftentimes the lay clergy can help. Or perhaps there's a church-run home for the baby."

"An orphanage."

"Mm." He looked thoughtful. "That's why St. Mary's was opened. To provide a place for children who are lacking certain religious guidance."

"Or lacking a propensity for it." She didn't mean to argue. Couldn't help but argue.

"Mm."

"Why aren't there any nuns at St. Mary's?"

"There are a couple, still."

"Oh." She didn't realize.

"What's the difference between a nun's work and a friar's?"

He cocked his head. "I'm glad you're asking questions. It's the first step in solidifying your faith."

She waited.

"A nun has a responsibility to the innocents and the helpless among us. The old, sick, and the young."

"And you don't?"

"We serve the unfortunate, support the parish, and educate others. Some of us also have vocations outside of the monastery."

"Vocations?"

"Other jobs or positions within the community. Or maybe we left one to serve here but might return one day."

"What was yours?" she asked.

He gave her a kind look. "I was a psychologist."

"You're a doctor?"

He nodded.

"Will you do that again someday?"

Brother smiled. "Only if I'm called to."

CHAPTER 15—CADENCE

Dr. Sanders—*Kirk*—answered on the first ring, and Cadence wasn't ready.

She fumbled through a lukewarm greeting. "Um, hi? Um, Kirk, this is Cadence?" Ugh. Cadence couldn't stand when women asked their own names. "Cadence Van Dam?"

"Of course. Cadence. Hi." His voice was warm and smooth as melted butter. "I'm so glad you called."

She remembered that she never did call him back after hanging up to deal with the charter school drama. "I'm sorry it wasn't sooner. Things have been a little crazy." Cadence winced. She hated cliches almost as much as she hated asking her name.

Kirk didn't notice, or he didn't mind. "So I've heard. Some hard stuff coming to light on this little island, huh?"

Hard stuff? Coming to light? Cadence hesitated. She was about to tell him that she just wanted to let him know that she no longer required his professional services but would he care to join her for a coffee one Saturday morning? But his tantalizing little address had her all mixed up about what she should say next. "Hard stuff?" She could make vague hints, too.

"The discovery at the build site." Ah. So Dr. Kirk Sanders wasn't a game player. Good for him.

And for Cadence.

"Right. And, yes. Very hard. St. Mary's is in the process of reaching out to offer some support right now." She wasn't trying to sound holier than thou, but it came out that way. Cadence was very good at building and keeping up walls, but something in her turned a little soft. She edited herself. "Well, to be honest, it's me. I'm going to get in touch with the admin team. I feel for them. The weather has already delayed the construction."

Kirk replied, "That's very good of you, Cadence."

She didn't need praise. "It's the right thing. And,

anyway, it's not only the new school this whole thing affects. It's the island at large. At least, I feel affected."

"Oh, of course. It's very personal, human suffering."

Cadence wondered if he knew more than she did. "Human suffering, right. Is that—did the police release new information?"

"You haven't heard?"

"Heard what?" Cadence was rapt now. It didn't matter that her class was about to return. It didn't matter that she was going to call Rutherford on her lunch period. Therapy and Kirk Sanders—nothing mattered. She quieted her breath and pushed the phone as tight to her ear as she could stand.

Kirk's reply came gently. "There was a press release a bit ago. Unfortunately, the person in question was likely the victim of foul play."

"Foul play?" Cadence's heart thumped in her chest.

"Yes. But, I hate to even discuss it. It feels...like gossip. Just a very sad, sad thing. And anyway, I'm sure you didn't call about that."

"Right," Cadence answered slowly. "I didn't call about that." But now she wanted that to be their topic of conversation. Instead, however, she went on, "I called about our last phone call. Or, I suppose, you had called me, but then I'd cut you off—"

"Oh, sure!" his tone brightened, and with it, Cadence's heart. Gone were the dull thumps. Instead, it fluttered. All of these inward feelings were coming back to life inside of her, and Cadence knew that it was because she'd found a new purpose. She was right to come back to St. Mary's. She was right to give up therapy. She was *happy*. Not herself, no. But happy.

"Again, I'm sorry I had to get off the phone," she said, waiting for him to explain why he'd called to begin with. Waiting for him to be the first to invite her for coffee. Waiting to accept.

Instead, however, he said, "That's right. I'd actually called as a follow-up for our meeting."

"Our meeting?" Had she already agreed to the coffee? Or was that a hope that had been living in her mind? "Our meeting, right," she tried to play along.

"I was wondering if we could plan for this coming Friday. From what I understand, St. Mary's lets out early on Fridays."

Encouraged by his intel on her place of employment and his assumption that she'd be free, she rushed to confirm. "Yes, that's right. We're done by noon! Mass in the morning, then a brief couple of hours before dismissal."

"Any chance you could come over at, say one? Is that too early? I'm not sure if you have after-school duties, or anything?"

She could hear the lingering hope in his voice, and it gave her every confidence that this was it. The start of their friendship. The next chapter in her happy life, even if it was a life she still wasn't quite used to. This was the beginning of becoming the new Cadence Van Dam. Maybe she'd even change her name. Take on that hyphen she'd once considered. Thoughts of her name scrawled out in great swooping letters clouded her brain momentarily. *Cadence Sageberry-Van Dam.* Or would it be better as *Cadence Sageberry Van Dam*, no hyphen? "No, no. One o'clock is perfect!" And it was made all the more perfect by the early hour. Just as coffee would have been casual and free from expectations, a late lunch get-together would be, too. Maybe he'd serve apps and tea.

"That's great. I'll pencil you in," he answered.

Cadence grinned to herself and flipped her own planner open. "I'll pencil you in, too."

And that was that. She could move on. She could

leave the horrors of the construction-site discovery and head straight into a weekend already filling up with happy distractions.

CHAPTER 16—DARLA

Back home after the shopping trip, Darla and Tatum were fixated on the TV. The babies had fallen asleep in the car seats on the way home, and it was in those carriers, which were now sitting in the middle of the living room, where they remained. The boys inside continued to snooze.

A regional news reporter appeared on the screen. Bundled in a heavy down coat, scarf, and hat, she gripped her microphone in a knit-gloved hand.

In the background of the shot, a place only marginally familiar to Darla and only because of recent events. A very partially framed out addition to an old building. The monastery that once was associated with St. Mary's parish. All together, the locale was where the new school was supposed to be built and, indeed, the building of which was underway.

But the construction was plainly arrested. Raw wood beams leaned into scaffolding. Heavy equipment sat unmoving in the periphery of the shot. Closer to where the reporter stood, yellow police tape. *DO NOT CROSS* shouted from the black print fluttering in a light breeze.

The reporter looked to have received a cue in her ear, and she began her broadcast.

"Thank you, Tim. This is Elena Martes reporting live from the so-called easternmost coast of Heirloom Island, a tiny sliver of land floating in the middle of Lake Huron. Some may know this area of Michigan if they've visited the popular tourist town of Birch Harbor, a mainland community just a ferry's ride west of where I stand today.

Others still know the name *Heirloom Island* indeed because of a grisly discovery made earlier this week just behind where I now stand." She gestured back.

Tatum, expression entirely glazed over, remarked, "Wow. We're famous."

"Luckily, *we* are not famous." Darla peeked over at the boys, who slumbered away. Precious moments. And peaceful ones, too.

"You know what I mean. Heirloom Island is famous, and since it's so small, that means anyone who lives here will be famous."

"When did you ever hear of a small town making people famous? And for such a dark thing?" But even as she asked her sister, who she figured wouldn't have an answer, examples popped up in Darla's mind. "I take that back."

"So there are some?" Tatum asked. "Small towns made famous by tragedy?"

"Chappaquiddick."

"Huh?" Tatum glanced at her. On the screen, the reporter recounted the basic details on the discovery.

Darla explained quickly. "One of the Kennedys died there. A car accident. And then there's Fall River. Home to Lizzie Borden. Tombstone—lot of death there, right?"

"And now Heirloom Island," Tatum added. "But it's just one set of human remains."

"Shh," Darla shushed her and raised the volume with the remote while the reporter's voice turned more somber.

"The police have only *just* announced the initial findings of the autopsy, which was conducted yesterday, late afternoon. According to the coroner's office, visible and obvious signs of trauma indicate the very clear suggestion that the woman—as we now know the remains are female—suffered foul play. Indeed, further information will confirm whether her death is the result of some violent act. In the meantime, local and county police have launched a comprehensive inquiry into the subject. Who was this woman, and why did she end up in a shallow grave on a small island in the middle of Lake Huron?"

The reporter returned the broadcast to the studio newscasters, and Darla lowered the volume back down. "Wow. It kind of freaks me out." She again looked in on the boys, who were beginning to rustle.

"Me, too. Maybe it's a serial killer."

"I doubt that," Darla said. And she did. "But it's obviously suspicious. And, well, *bad*."

"Do you think it had to do with the monastery?"

"I don't know. Maybe they can date the remains and find out about when she passed? I thought the monastery had been closed for a long time." Darla lifted Shep out of his carrier and set him up with a bottle in Tatum's arms then did the same with Gabriel.

"Have you heard from Rip today?" Darla asked. "Maybe he's got more information?"

Tatum answered, "Briefly. He texts me a lot, but it's never anything important." She sounded petulant. Angry, even.

"What do you mean?"

"He'll say hi and see how I'm doing. That's all he's done today." She didn't look at Darla.

"Did he come to the island today?"

"No. He says there wasn't a point in him coming today, since the project's on hold."

Tatum's pain was plain as day. Darla hadn't so far encouraged a romance between Tatum and their very own in-law. It felt incestuous, even if it wasn't. And anyway, Tatum wasn't ready to date. Not by Darla's standards. Were Darla's standards too high?

Maybe. She snuggled Gabe deeper into her arm and eased farther back on the sofa. "Tatum, have you thought about making the first move?"

"What first move? The first move has already been made. We've gone on dates. We've kissed. It's out there. It's just...not going anywhere, I guess."

"I'm not an expert on dating, but—"

"You've had one serious relationship, and you ended it. And now you have his twins, and he's ready to sign his parental rights away."

Darla tried not to wince from the brutal points. But she did have to correct Tatum. "Hunter already signed his rights away." It was sad, really. The fact that Hunter had no interest in his sons. Sad for the boys. Sad for Darla. And, even, sad for Hunter. Darla wondered what it would be like for Shep and Gabriel to grow up without a dad. Would it be bad? Would they turn out to be problem kids? The products of a broken family that broke even before they were born? She prayed every night that they'd be okay. That they could do without a father or even a father figure, because Darla was staunch in her refusal to be *that* woman. The mother who let strangers in and forced her children to call every third date Dad. She shuddered at the thought.

But then, Tatum wasn't a mother, not even a single mother. She could afford to have fun. And it was plain as could be that she wanted to have fun with Rip. Darla *should* be encouraging this. "Anyway, Hunter is not the only man I ever dated. And I'm not going to defend what little advice I have to offer. So take this or leave it, okay?"

"Okay." Tatum looked at her with puppy dog eyes, like it was Rip she was staring at, and not her sister. She had it bad. That was for sure.

"You're both adults. He is clearly interested in you. Interested enough to text and bring you coffee and take you out. And if you want to be exclusive with him, then you have the right to ask him if he feels the same way. That's what you want, right? Commitment?"

Tatum's eyes grew wide and she shook her head adamantly. "No, no, no. I don't need commitment. I don't even want commitment. Commitment is the last thing in the world I need or want, actually. Definitely not that."

Darla laughed a little. "Okay, then what is it? What is it you want to have with Rip?"

A quizzical look washed over Tatum's delicate features, adding a gravity to her messy, staticky black hair and bright green eyes that needed no makeup to shine like a pair of gems. Her thin lips, too—all of it was darkened by some deep thought or fear. Like Cadence, it was as though a sense of dread had descended on Tatum. "Tatum, what is it? What's wrong?"

Tatum snapped out of it and met Darla's stare. "I don't know. I don't know what I want."

"Really?" Darla asked. "Because it seems to me like you know exactly what you want. And *who*."

CHAPTER 17—TATUM

Tatum left the boardwalk to return home. The Manger House was home now, despite the fact that she had never made the official announcement that it was.

And yet, even though she'd brought her dream to life, something was off. Maybe it was the problem of not enough intakes. Winter on the island was destined to be a slow time, and that wasn't a bad thing. It was good that animals had found their own shelters somewhere—maybe even in people's homes. The problem was, however, it meant there wasn't much to draw in money. And, there wasn't much to do.

Once all the animals were fed and watered and taken out and brushed, and once the dishes were put away and the bed was turned down, Tatum realized she didn't even have a television to watch. She might as well be living in the year 1900 on a farm. A snowy farm in the dead of winter, without someone to chop and bring in the wood or stoke the fire. A forced-air furnace didn't add the same coziness as Tatum had grown up with. She'd grown up with a dad who chopped wood and made a great fire. A mother who braided the girls' hair before bed so they'd wake up with crimps in it. She'd grown up, too, with a set of older sisters who loved her. Who teased her and loved her. And then there were the slow stream of family pets.

Pets had always felt like Tatum's haven—her safety net of affection. When feeling lonesome, she could snuggle up next to Angus on the floor, if need be. More often than not, though, the others would jump up on the bed and join her, and they'd keep each other warm. And it was enough. And knowing that Tatum could now help other animals in need of a home find that same warmth, it was that dream.

But what was a girl to do once she'd achieved her dream?

What came next?

This was the predicament in which Tatum presently found herself. A good predicament to have, no doubt. But a predicament nonetheless.

She slipped down deep beneath layers of blankets on her bed. She'd found her phone at some point in the week, and it was charging at her bedside table. Seeing it there now made her feel neat and organized and like a grown-up. Tatum hated that. She hated thinking of herself as a *grown-up* or an adult. It was silly. She *was* an adult. She *was* grown up. And even some grown-ups weren't attached to their phones. So what if Tatum wasn't? Maybe it even made her better in some way, that she didn't rely upon technology for entertainment and communication. She didn't rely on technology to foster her relationships. To nurture them.

She popped the charging cord from its port and turned the device on. Once it woke up, she saw that she'd missed text messages from Rip. The last they'd talked was that morning. His usual Good Morning message and her usual Good Morning response and then, nothing much else apart from his point that he wouldn't be coming to the island today because there was no point in it.

But now, she saw that he did have something else to say. A lot more, in fact.

She frowned and read through three separate texts.

If you need anything from the mainland, let me know! I can always make a special trip.

Just checking to see if you read the news. Tatum, be sure to lock your doors. Who knows when that poor woman met her death. And who did it. Could be a crazy on the island. Lock your doors, okay?

Lastly: *Getting worried I haven't heard from you. Please call or write back soon. Going to reach out to your sisters if I don't hear back...*

Tatum glanced at the timestamp of the last text. It came in just ten minutes before.

She tapped Rip's name and put a call to him right away. No sense in worrying the poor thing. She hated to worry people, and yet it seemed like she was doing it more and more often.

"Tatum?" he answered right away. "Are you okay?"

"I'm fine! I'm fine. I'm sorry I worried you. I didn't have my phone with me today."

"Oh, thank God. I—listen, I don't know why but once I got news about the body they found and the fact that it might have been murder, I just, I sort of freaked out. I should have tried harder to get in touch with you earlier today. I waited too long. I'm so sorry. I'm—I'm talking too much." He fell quiet, and Tatum grinned to herself.

"No, you're not. I like hearing your voice." She felt bold, in the depths of her blankets, surrounded on either side of her bed by her furbabies.

"You do?" his voice turned gravelly, and it made Tatum squirm under the sheets.

"I love your voice, actually." She swallowed and held her breath. Had she gone too far? Flirted too hard?

"Well, that's a coincidence."

"It is?" she squeaked.

He laughed. "Because I like your voice, too. I love it. Even when you sound like a mouse."

She cleared her throat. "Is there anything else you happen to like about me?" Very bold.

"Are you kidding me, Tatum? What *don't* I like about you?" He chuckled, and she realized that she'd never heard someone actually chuckle. She liked it. Which meant she liked Rip's voice and his laugh. And his arms and Adam's apple and the way he was so kind to her and kind to animals and—*sigh*.

"Oh?" she was fishing, and hard, but Tatum never fished for compliments, and she never flirted. This was...fun.

"I like your personality. I like what you do with

your life and how you are with your sisters. How you love animals, well, obviously I like that. I like the way you look." He chuckled again. "A lot."

Tatum felt herself grow hot in the face. "You like how I look? I'm not, dorky looking?"

"No way. You're so cute." Another chuckle. "Actually, you're really pretty, Tatum. I thought that since I met you. You're, um, well, you're beautiful."

A tight quiet cinched them together on the phone line. She could almost hear his breath in the receiver. Or was it hers?

"I like how fun you are, and funny. How you mix up expressions. It's adorable. You're adorable. You're —well—I just *really* like you. But, you know all this. Right?"

"I mean," Tatum licked her lips and gave Angus a scruff behind the ear. He sat right at her bedside, practically panting along with her. "No?"

"I like you a lot."

"I just guess I got confused because you didn't want to come over last night, and we don't really talk about what we're *doing*. You know?"

In the distance of his end of the line, she could hear a door close. A car or a truck door maybe.

She stopped herself from going on. "What was that?"

"What?" he asked.

"Where are you?" the skin on her spine tingled. Tatum had never in her life been a jealous person. She'd never had cause to be jealous. There'd never been anything to be jealous of, for goodness' sake. But what was the noise? Where was he so late at night? And why was he there?

"Where am I?" he repeated back to her.

Tatum scowled and sat up in her bed, now on high alert. "Yeah. Where are you? I heard a door close."

"That's the thing, Tatum. This is ridiculous and so awkward."

"What is it?" she demanded. Angus started barking, but it wasn't at her or the phone call. He was moving away from her and heading out of the bedroom.

Rip answered, "I'm here."

"Here?" Tatum almost dropped the phone. "Here, *where*?"

"At your place?" he answered bashfully. "Sorry— I was on my way once I didn't hear from you. I just, I was worried."

"Okay." Tatum digested this. It was good. All of it, good. He worried about her. He cared about her. He came.

But, should he stay? And if he did, what would happen?

"If you're safe, though," Rip went on, "I can go. I don't want to bother you."

"No. I'm glad you came." She was throwing back the covers and scrambling for something to throw on over her jammies. A cute robe—she didn't have one. A cute beanie—she didn't know where she'd thrown it. "I just, I'm not exactly dressed."

"Not dressed?" His tone was nothing short of suggestive, and Tatum immediately corrected him.

"I mean, I'm in my pajamas. I'm not naked." A nervous laugh bubbled up and erupted from Tatum. "This is awkward. I just—I'll be right there." She hung up and found an old hoodie to pull on, over her ratty PJ top. The last thing she wanted was for Rip to see her in rags. Not that the hoodie was much better, but at least it didn't have holes. On the bottom, she wore soft flannel pants that would have to do. She pushed her feet into fuzzy slippers and pulled her hair up in a half-pony. All together, Tatum probably looked like, well, Tatum, honestly. She accepted this and went to the door.

Rip stood in a blue puffer jacket with a blue hat and black gloves on his hands, which poked out of the jacket pockets on either side. His expression lifted into a full-faced smile when he saw her.

"Hi," she said, only moderately self conscious of her appearance. But then Rip leaned forward, his arms outstretched and pulled Tatum in for a hug, and all insecurities fizzled away.

He nuzzled her neck and whispered back, "Hi."

Once inside, Tatum set about whipping up two mugs of hot cocoa topped in whipped cream and marshmallows. Rip, meanwhile, gave the dogs each a rub down.

"I'm glad you came," Tatum confessed. "I had wished that—" but she thought better of it. Last night was then. Tonight was now.

Rip, though, wouldn't let her let it go. "You wished what?"

She brought him his drink and they went to the living room, where a comfortable, well worn sofa sat facing the fireplace. Rip tugged a chenille blanket from the armchair and pulled it across their laps as they lowered together with their drinks. The dogs settled in front of the fireplace, which had nothing more than a layer of dwindling embers from the fire Tatum had made earlier in the evening.

"This is my idea of a perfect night," Rip said as he took a long sip of his cocoa then set it down. She did the same with hers before she noticed that a foam mustache had emerged across his upper lip.

Tatum laughed and pointed. "You're like the cute guy from a romantic comedy. You've got something on your—" she moved her finger closer to his lips, and his eyes lost their smile. She fell serious, too.

Rip ran his tongue up and over the whipped cream, and just as soon as it had appeared, it was gone. Tatum was left to stare at his bare lips, full and soft and daring her to press her mouth against them.

Not one to normally overthink things, she closed her eyes and leaned in, and to her great joy, Rip did the same. He twisted towards her, both his hands cupping her face. Tatum turned into him, too, until she was nearly in his lap. Her hands gripped the back of Rip's neck, and they moved to the kisses in time. It was a dance, their kissing, and many irresistible moments later, when they finally parted for a breath, Tatum felt her face flush anew under his gaze.

They fell asleep there, chastely spooned against each other—as chastely as such cuddling could be. And while Tatum hadn't wanted Rip to sleep so close to her and so soon, she found herself happy to wake up in his arms.

CHAPTER 18—CADENCE

As the week pressed on, Cadence grew busier and busier. Her self-imposed outreach effort to Mr. Rutherford and team continued to fall on a back-burner. And anyway, Cadence had to give the police another couple of days to wrap up their evidence collection and finish their excavation. There was no sense in getting in the way. But things were looking up as Friday morning rolled around and the police tape was pulled from the construction site. According to the news, there were no other remains to be found at what would become the subfloor for the new school.

Of course, even using that phrasing—remains to be found at the new school—was giving the public fits about how the new charter school could even move forward knowing what had been there, on the property.

As public scrutiny heated up, Cadence made a point to call Mr. Rutherford that morning before classes began. She figured she could offer him a kindness and assurance that this, too, should pass. And if they needed anything, the doors to St. Mary's were wide open. Sincerely.

She put the call through.

He answered after several rings. "Roger Rutherford speaking." His voice was gruff and terse, but Cadence reminded herself that he was under great stress and pressure. He needed grace, not judgment.

"Hello, Mr. Rutherford. You don't know me, but my name is Cadence Van Dam. I'm a teacher and community member here on the island."

No answer came.

She went on. "Anyway," as brightly as she could, "I'm calling to reach out on behalf of St. Mary's Catholic School."

"Ah, yes. St. Mary's Catholic School." Now she heard it loudly and clearly. His voice was worse than gruff and terse. It was brusque and rude, too. But it wasn't only in his voice that his derision became evident. His words pricked like needles. "Of course.

The people we were supposed to be putting out of business."

Shocked, Cadence had but one thing with which to reply. "I beg your pardon?"

"Beg all you want. I know exactly who's behind this skeleton business, and it's the Church." He laughed disdainfully. "They always were. Ever since I left the faith, the Church has been on my back in one way, shape, or form. Why do you think I brought my vision to the island? To save those kids."

"Save our kids? From what, may I ask?"

"From the evils of the bishop and the Pope themselves, of course. And whatever funny old priest you have lording over your parish." He snorted. "Mark my words, we'll learn soon enough that you people *planted* that poor woman at our work site. I know conflict of interest when I see it. And I saw it yesterday!"

"I have no idea what you're talking about, Mr. Rutherford. But if you'd take a moment to let me talk, you'd know I called you today to offer my help. Not to rub this in your face or to be the victim of your verbal attack." Cadence seethed. "Indeed, I don't tolerate this sort of treatment. So, while I won't rescind my offer to the likes of your fledgling faculty and staff, I will, however, end our phone call now. If you wish to accept our help or if your staff needs anything, please have *someone else* call."

He wasn't done with her yet. "Someone else? Oh, sure. Like your brother? Rip Van Dam? He could call for us. Or even better, how about his girlfriend? She's your sister? This town is nothing short of an isle of inbreeding. You people disgust me."

"And your behavior, Mr. Rutherford, disgusts *me*. Good*bye*." Cadence hung up and fell into her seat, defeated and shaking. What in the world was that about? What had happened with Rip? And Tatum, presumably? And this poor man's bad experiences in the Catholic church? It was as though he was chomping at the bit to take someone out, and that someone was Cadence. At least, this morning it was. Although, deep down she knew she wasn't his target.

Mr. Rutherford's target was the truth. The truth that his precious charter school project was stalled out. The truth that he might not be able to start a new school year next fall.

And the truth that he had a school full of personnel who may be on unemployment come August.

CHAPTER 19—DARLA

Darla was scrolling through a page of remote job listings when her phone rang Friday morning.

Cadence.

"Hey. Is Tatum there?" Cadence asked. She sounded like she was in a hurry.

"No, why?"

"Do you know if she was at the construction site yesterday? With Rip?"

"I have no idea. Isn't it still a crime scene? And again, *why*?"

Cadence huffed into the line. "I just got off the phone with the principal of the new school. I guess Rip and Tatum were there, and for whatever reason, it gave him a bad taste about me and St. Mary's. Or maybe, the bad taste was always there. He was exceedingly rude. So much so that I'm a little shaken up, to be honest."

Darla pushed the laptop away and gave her sister her full attention. "Are you okay? What exactly did he say?"

"He went off on the church, for starters."

"Well, that's personal. It has nothing to do with you."

"Right, and that's fine, I guess. But then he basically said we are all a bunch of inbreds, and he suggested that Rip and Tatum are out at the site scouting on my behalf, or maybe St. Mary's? I don't know. It was crazy talk. Super upsetting. He was so enraged. And it seemed like he was enraged at me."

"Ouch, well. He's got to be under a ton of pressure right now." Darla could easily be the voice of reason for someone else. But when it came to her own troubles, she was a little less effectual. Like right before Cadence called, when she opened about a bajillion tabs on her computer, each with a random remote job that would never in a million years be something she would want to do or be qualified to do... Darla pulled the laptop back to her and exited out of the Internet all together. She couldn't deal with a job search right now. Not *reasonably*, at least.

"Of course," Cadence answered. "And I get that,

but it doesn't give him the right to all-out attack me. He implied that St. Mary's staged the whole thing."

"What whole thing?"

"The discovery of the body. He suggested that there was never a body there to begin with, and that we brought in a body! That we set it up to stall his construction."

Darla laughed. It was comical, really. The sort of thing that would happen in a dark comedy or a cozy mystery or kooky old horror film with an oddball ending. Not reality. He was off his rocker, this Rutherford guy. Darla said as much.

"I agree, but I mean, I get it, too." Cadence sounded beaten.

Darla tried to sympathize. "We have no details about the remains. For all anyone knows, it's the body of a nun who wished to be buried at the old monastery, right?"

"Why would a nun be buried there. Monasteries are for monks. Monks lived there. Not nuns."

"Nuns probably visited. Or maybe they had retreats there? You know?"

"I don't know an abbey anywhere in Michigan, much less around here. I don't think it was a nun."

"Or a secretary? Monasteries probably had female secretaries or something."

"I think it's bad business, whatever happened. I don't think it's some innocent thing, and that makes this mess all the messier, Darla."

Darla hated to hear her sister so upset. "Okay, fair. But it isn't our mess, Cade. Or yours, for that matter."

"It kind of is. It's affecting Rip, and he's family. And Tatum is involved? Why?"

"She's not answering her phone?" Darla asked.

"Of course not."

"Well, I mean, you have two choices," Darla pointed out.

"What are those?"

"One, wait and see. Let things blow over. Or two, intervene."

"I just tried to intervene. I got called an inbred," Cadence said flatly.

Darla tried hard to hold back her laughter, but it was hard to do in the face of utter ridiculousness. It burst out.

"How is this funny?" But the humor came through in Cadence's voice, too, and soon they were both laughing. After a moment, Cadence stopped and said, "I have class starting soon. I don't think there's another possible intervention with this guy."

"You could invite him and his team and the team

at St. Mary's over for a Come-to-Jesus, of sorts," Darla suggested.

"What?"

"Like, a town hall. The two schools get together. Problem solve. Maybe there's a way through this for the new charter and St. Mary's can be of real help, after all? Maybe it just needs to be more formal than an off-hand phone call. You know?"

"Like an event? Sounds a little much to me. And anyway, I'm not sure I have it in me to organize something like that."

At this, Darla frowned. "But, it's your side hustle, Cade. Your business is doing events on the board-walk, right?" She tried for light laughter, but it came out strangled, and a fresh awkwardness filled the phone line.

"Right, I know." Cadence sounded defensive. "It's just bad timing. This is all way too crazy."

"You *are* going to do events, though. Right?"

"Why?"

Darla could practically picture her older sister bristling.

She bristled, herself. "Because, um, *money*?"

"I'm teaching again. And we have the rental now. I think we're set, Darla." But her tone offered no reassurance and only restrained irritation. Darla felt funny about it all.

"Well, I want to be able to contribute, and I can help put on events, Cadence."

"Darla, don't be silly. You do contribute. You take care of the house. It's fine. Listen, I have to go now. Talk later, okay?"

With that, the conversation was over.

And Darla was back online, searching for jobs that belonged to other people. People who had degrees in something other than the troubled world of education.

CHAPTER 20—TATUM

That week, Rip and Tatum were inseparable. He hadn't stayed the night again, no. But he'd come to the island every day, stopping first at Tatum's and rejoining her for lunch and then dinner. They hadn't talked about what it was they were doing yet, but Tatum was content in the attention Rip lavished upon her. More than content.

Thursday afternoon, Rip had asked if she wanted to go to the site with him. The crime scene was cleared, and he was supposed to meet Mr. Rutherford and Mr. Chamberlain for a walk-through and to discuss a game plan.

Tatum had asked him why she ought to go. She knew nothing about the project, effectively, and wouldn't it be odd?

But Rip had brushed her concerns aside easily, arguing it was informal, and afterwards, they could go to the mainland for a special dinner. That way, he wouldn't need to drive back down to the southern coast of Heirloom. It'd give them more time together, too. And Tatum had nothing but time. Especially since she'd re-homed both her fosters the day before.

But not only did she have time, Tatum had a reason to go into Birch Harbor Thursday night. After dinner, Rip was taking her to meet Mason Acton at the high school for a spring planning committee of which he was currently overseeing. The school was looking for booth representatives for their upcoming bizarre. The fee was nominal and they liked to see both vendors and local non-profit organizations.

The new animal shelter was sure to be a hit. Tatum could bring informational brochures and animals available for adoption. She could also get the word out that people were welcome to contact her if they came across any strays on the mainland. She had a ferry for transportation and could house even more dogs and cats than the nearest mainland shelter.

So, come time, Rip picked Tatum up. She snuggled next to him in his truck, and off they went to the work site. Once there, introductions were made, and as far as Tatum could tell, everything went normally. Rutherford wasn't exactly the friendliest guy she'd ever met, but Tatum quickly learned why. The school was in danger of falling off schedule. Even one week in January could pose a problem for their planned opening date of August 1. But this delay would last longer than a week.

The school's board was holding a special meeting to discuss the considerations for and repercussions of plowing ahead in light of the discovery.

Rutherford had even said to Rip, "If you can't make this mess go away, Van Dam, then we'll sue you for damages and find a contractor more able to handle everything."

Tatum had been impressed that Rip was unflinching in his reply. "You'd be in breach of contract, which would put us back on level playing ground, Roger. But if you wish to take that action, no one's stopping you. Least of all St. Mary's, I'm sure."

Tatum hadn't exactly understood this threat at first.

It was only later, when they were taking Rip's boat across the lake to the mainland that she'd asked him about it. "What did you mean earlier? About no one stopping Mr. Rutherford and St. Mary's? I didn't get it."

"I just mean that it's not like many people are exactly gunning for the guy's success. I've heard even his own board is ready to pull the plug on the operation. Apparently, they were never exactly on board with the location, anyway. It's been fraught."

Tatum had frowned. "But St. Mary's doesn't want him to fail, and they don't want him to sue you, I'm sure. Right?"

"I just meant that this guy thinks St. Mary's wished tragedy on him and the project, and it isn't true. If he goes forth with suing anyone, St. Mary's isn't going to get in his way, just as they were never trying to get in his way to begin with."

Tatum had still been a little confused, but she was also assured by Rip's good heartedness and earnestness. With every time she spoke with him, she was more and more confident that this wasn't just a crush. Maybe it was more.

They'd gotten to the mainland in time for the meeting to begin, and Mason had introduced Tatum and her organization—The Manger House. The folks at the meeting had given her a hearty and warm welcome, and Tatum felt good.

After the meeting, Mason had invited Tatum and

Rip for drinks at some dive bar further north. At first, Tatum had declined, citing her animals back home who needed to go out and her own exhaustion from a week full of craziness. But actually, she'd declined because she'd been hoping she might persuade Rip to cuddle with her on the sofa again. Maybe fall asleep with her again. Maybe wake up with her again and they could talk about the trajectory of things again.

But Rip had other ideas. "Let's go, Tate. The dogs are okay. They can last another hour or two, right?"

At that, Tatum had felt a little dejected. Her romantic interest was opting to grab drinks with his friend, and Tatum could come along as a third wheel. It shot her confidence in where they were going, but counterintuitively, it also served to pique Tatum's interest even more, if that were possible.

Apparently it was, because the minute they'd stepped into the bar, she'd felt desperately attracted to Rip. She'd watched him with renewed thirst as he'd ordered her favorite drink—a fuzzy navel—and gulped his own beer. She'd watched him as he bought the trio a second round, clinking his foamy-topped drink with Mason's as they laughed at an old memory and launched into a new one.

Tatum had found that she didn't even mind just

listening in on their inside jokes. There was something in Rip's way that made her feel included despite being the outsider. In fact, she felt like she was the center of his world, even as every conversation overlapped more with Mason. And Mason, to his credit, included Tatum, too. He asked after the animals. He asked after Cadence, and her venue business. Tatum was a little awkward to tell him it hadn't yet taken off. And by night's end, Mason had asked, too, after Darla.

The anticipation in his question had been palpable, but the nervousness was there, too. Especially when he'd asked, his voice slick with drink but his words wobbly with desperation. "Has she, like, *asked*, about me or anything, Tatum?"

"Oh, um." Tatum had stopped after two, and so she'd been more able to process what he meant. It had come quickly, too, her awareness that Mason had it bad for Darla. This had made an impact on Tatum. Darla had just had babies. Two of them. At once! And Mason wanted to know if she was thinking about him? And anyway, if Darla *was* to ask about Mason, why would she ask Tatum?

"I think his question is for me," Rip had said, "but he's asking you so that you'll report back to your sister that he asked."

Tatum gave her head a clearing shake. "Okay, well, to answer you, Mason, she certainly hasn't asked me about you. But then again, she's pretty busy."

"Is she back teaching?" he'd asked, unfazed by the relative dejection.

"Oh, no." Tatum didn't realize Mason was so out of the loop, but then again Darla's decision to stay home for the second semester was new. She'd even caught her own principal off guard. "She's home. With the boys. Cadence went back, though."

"That's great for Darla," Mason replied. His eyes looked a little misty, like he really was happy for her. Or he really had drunk too much, maybe. "I'm happy for her."

"She's happy. A little stressed about finances, but happy." Tatum had instantly regretted saying so much. "But, I mean, she's fine. We're all fine!" Tatum laughed nervously.

Mason's face twisted, though. It was though the alcohol drained from his blood and with one shake of his head, he was thinking clearly, Worriedly. They were outside now, in the frigid night air. Rip's arm wrapped around Tatum, and Mason stood apart from them, his hands shoved deep in his pockets.

Shoulders hunched. "Is she going to go back to teaching?"

Tatum was too cold and now too embarrassed to continue this conversation. Plus, she had no idea what Darla's long-term plans were. She shrugged, though the gesture was likely lost to the layers of her outerwear and Rip's arm and the dark sky around them.

Mason and Rip made their goodbyes and the trio headed for the parking lot. But before each set parted ways for good, Mason called over to Tatum, "If she wants to go back to teaching, I know an open position at the high school."

But he didn't get it. Darla couldn't take a teaching job. She wanted to be home. How could she possibly be a teacher *and* stay home? Tatum knew the sad truth. Darla was stuck. And even the handsome Mason Acton couldn't shake her free.

CHAPTER 21—CADENCE

The school day dragged on more slowly than any Friday ever had. Probably because Cadence was going to Kirk's house after school for tea and a light, late lunch. She felt so fanciful, meeting a new friend —a male friend—for a platonic get-together in his lakeside home. Cadence also had the sense that everything, almost, was right in the world as she finished her school day. Wiping the desks down, slotting books back into their spots on the shelf, and clearing her desk took no more than five minutes. But once she packed her school tote, time slowed. Cadence found herself all but stalling as she tucked every last grade-able paper into her folio, checked that her pack of gum and compact and lip gloss were in their little pouch in front, glanced around the room one last time, turned off the lights, then closed the door, locking it manually from the outside.

She pressed a hand against the door and then leaned into it, stilling herself for a moment.

And then, she left for Kirk's house.

The drive was pleasant, the car warm, pop hits playing on the car radio. Hendrik had always hated pop music. Maybe because he was older or maybe because his taste was more refined, he preferred classics, jazz. That sort of thing. Cadence hadn't had much interest in music since his death, and even during his life and the life of their marriage, she was indifferent. But something about singing along to songs that she heard the girls play when they lived at home, the songs that department stores played and even the Bait Shop, it pepped her up. Made her feel young. Made her feel her age, actually.

After she rolled up the short drive of the Sanders' house on the lake, Cadence checked her reflection in the drop-down vanity. Her face was flushed from the singing and the warmth of the car. Her eyes were bright. Her mouth needed a little color. She swabbed some of her lip gloss on, smacked her lips together.

Her phone buzzed from her purse. Worry shot up her chest. Maybe it was Kirk, texting her from inside to cancel.

That would be fine, of course. He could cancel. He had every right. They were friends, and friends understood last-minute cancellations. Or, even if they weren't yet friends, they were on their way. And it'd be just fabulous, too. Cadence would much rather have Kirk as a friend than as a therapist. She didn't need therapy. Look at her. Here she was, driving from school to the lake playing pop music and singing all the way. She was reborn. The tragedy at the new school site had pushed a button in Cadence. Reminded her that life was short. That you never knew when it'd be your turn.

This revelation might have occurred to her when she was sitting at Hendrik's deathbed, watching him wither away. But then, she was too close.

The person found at the construction site was probably a complete stranger. It was far easier to think of that person as a singular, unconnected example of the fleeting thing that was life. Rather than to think of that person as someone she might know.

Someone she might mourn.

Someone whose death might matter to Cadence. *Really* matter.

Kirk's door opened for Cadence, and she beamed. "Hi!"

"Cadence." He looked relaxed but neat in a pale blue sweater over a checker-printed button-down and relaxed-fit khakis. On his feet, brown loafers. Kirk smiled and gestured toward the sofa and chair they'd sat in the last time she was in his home, for her first-ever therapy appointment.

She let out a little sigh of relief that she wouldn't be talking about her feelings with him, after all. Not her real ones at least.

Tugging her scarf loose from her neck and slipping from her coat, she passed both to Kirk, who hung them on the spindly rack by the door. Again, he lifted a hand to the sofa, and she made her way there, searching the coffee table and nearby side table for hints of what they might be eating with their tea. Nothing set out, yet.

Before she lowered down into the supple cushions, she asked, "Do you need help with anything, first?"

He gave her a funny look but quickly nodded. "No. Of course not. Please, have a seat."

She did, smiling all the while. Instead of sitting on the edge of the sofa, she let herself sink back. This was how friends were to act. Comfortable.

Kirk didn't head into the kitchen. He sat in the armchair, rather. Cadence frowned briefly at this. Shouldn't he be getting their tea? But that was okay. Maybe he had something he wanted to say first.

Cadence laced her fingers around one knee, and crossed it over the other. "I don't know if I said this before, but you have a beautiful home here, Kirk."

He adjusted his eyeglasses and gave a soft sort of smile. "Thank you." Then he looked about himself. "You know, when I was married, I didn't get to spend any time here at all."

"Oh?" Cadence wished she had that tea to sip. She let go of her leg and ran her hands down her thighs awkwardly.

As though he could read her mind, he lifted a hand. "I'm sorry. I didn't offer you a drink. Water?"

Water?

She blinked. "Um, sure. Thanks." He pushed up and swiveled around to the kitchen. Cadence chalked all of this up to Kirk's being a man. It was either that or something far worse.

Either Kirk wasn't entirely good at hosting a friend for tea and late lunch, *or* he was nervous.

And if he was nervous, then it could mean only one other thing.

That Dr. Kirk Sanders hadn't invited Cadence there on the promise of friendship. He'd invited her for another reason.

Because he was *interested*.

CHAPTER 22

Their couple sessions were growing shorter, and her private lessons grew deeper. Soon, her husband was staying just twenty minutes, for prayer and a brief discussion on how their homework had been going.

Marriage homework was the worst kind of homework. Forced dates and scheduled sex made both things feel like chores. And when both things already felt like chores before, well, it just got worse.

During the sixth session, and after six weeks of unsuccessful or incomplete marriage homework, the husband left. This time, though, in a huff. "This isn't working," he said in hushed tones to Brother.

"Sometimes, the work is happening deep down. It can take a long time to see the fruits of one's labor.

Think of an apple tree, planted as a sapling. One must monitor and water it, add mulch. Cover it on the coldest winter nights to ward off frost. Then, the next year, it will have grown, bit by bit. But will it flower? Not yet. And the cycle repeats, and it may not be years until that apple tree bears its first fruit."

She had something to say about this analogy. "It's flawed."

Both men looked at her in surprise.

She explained. "If that were true, then apple trees wouldn't grow wild in the countryside. There are apple trees and wildflowers that thrive without any maintenance at all."

"You think God doesn't provide that maintenance." Brother said this plainly.

"What?"

"In your own backyard, you are tending to your apple trees. In the countryside, it's God who blows fresh soil over a newly dropped seed. It's God who opens the sky to rain down on the seeds, the saplings, the old trees. God who protects them."

The husband cleared his throat. "So if you can't take care of your own apple trees, you let God take over."

Brother smiled. "That's why you're here."

She frowned. "Then why do we have to schedule date nights?"

ONCE HER HUSBAND had left and it was just the two of them, the wife and monk, she broached the topic from some weeks back.

Vocation.

"How did you know you were called to psychology? Or to the brotherhood, for that matter?" She'd always been interested in how people pinned down what it was they wanted to do with their lives. She wondered it for her husband, who was born into his vocation, effectively. A family with money and property. She wondered it for her children, all of whom so far seemed to march to their own beats.

"Some things, I sincerely believe, are passed down from generation to generation. Our bloodline is fraught with shrinks." He chuckled.

She thought about this. "That's not really a calling, then."

"I think there's more to it than that. And anyway, I left to pursue my Holy Orders."

"Now *that's* a calling."

His eyebrows fell low, and a slow smile crept over his face. "Oh? How do you mean?"

"I mean, it's not passed down, right? If you're a monk or a nun or a priest or whatever, it's not like your parents were. I just think that if you have a desire to serve the church, it comes from someplace deep down." She licked her lips and glanced around the barren wood room. It wasn't so bad in there. Nothing to distract her. Nothing to churn up her already-too-busy mind. Just wood. Just space.

Peace.

CHAPTER 23—DARLA

Friday, the sisters were supposed to have a late family dinner at home. Darla was doing the cooking. Tatum was supposed to come early to help with the boys. Cadence would set up and help in the kitchen.

Darla wanted to make something fancy. She felt distinctly and pleasantly refreshed at the end of the week, and it would make sense to take advantage and go all out. Darla wasn't usually the cook, and less so since the boys had come along.

Cadence wasn't expected until after three, and Tatum not until five since she kept regular operating hours at the shelter. It was only just after one now, and Darla had spent the better part of the day alternating between tending to the boys' needs and getting the kitchen and dining room as pulled together as she could manage. But a break was much needed, and her stomach grumbled with the pains of a postpartum hunger.

A quick bowl of cereal would do the trick, and with the babies fast asleep, Darla set herself up at the bar with the laptop and the bowl of Cheerios. She scrolled aimlessly through more job boards, on the hunt still. Everything labeled remote carried some degree of allure to Darla. Data entry— simple. Maybe even therapeutic, who knew? Medical billing—came with medical benefits which was, well, a huge benefit. Web design fascinated Darla, but it was too far out in left field. She'd need training at minimum. Maybe even a degree.

Her eyes skimmed down the page. Down, down, down, landing at last on a job posting that appealed to her a great deal, and one which she had a modicum of experience in.

Virtual coordinator for events business.

She skimmed the details. *Wanted: Applicant with experience in the coordination and organization of in-person events. Most work can be completed virtually or remotely, but position requires in-person presence approximately twenty percent, during the events. All coordination and organization are managed through online communication programs, including email and asynchronous software systems.*

This was all fancy talk for putting something together and showing up when it was time to show up. Darla could do all this. She could even plug their boardwalk venue.

Darla moved the mouse until the cursor hovered over the *Apply Now* icon.

Yes, Darla could do this.

But did she want to?

Not really.

Darla shut the computer and rubbed her eyes. Then, her phone pinged on the countertop. A soft beep reserved for text notifications from a select few of her contacts. Her sisters. Her mom. And one other person. Not because he was important, but because Darla often wondered if he would ever reach out to her again.

Turns out, he would. And now, he did.

Mason Acton's text was brief but compelling. *Did you hear the news?*

A perfectly vague hook to drag Darla back into his orbit. She pursed her lips at the words. No matter how she replied, it'd invite a continuation of this conversation. The problem with that was the fact that this conversation could not continue. It couldn't even start. Small talk had a way of turning into big talk, and the last thing Darla needed was to dive into deep waters with Mason Acton. Especially what with Valentine's Day coming up.

Darla slapped her forehead with the palm of her hand. Valentine's Day was over a month away. Ridiculous. *Ridiculous!* To think she'd celebrate Valentine's with any male other than her two boys was not only laughable, it was scandalous. In Darla's mind, dating would have to wait eighteen years, until the boys were out of the house. That was only proper.

Eighteen years.

It felt like forever. She stared again at his words. News. What news? She wrote him back. *Nope. What news?*

His reply came almost instantly. *They identified the remains from the construction site out on Heirloom.*

Darla's curiosity was duly whet now. She pushed herself further, silently cursing the fact that this conversation had never even started as small talk. It was only big talk. At least it wasn't personal talk though. News related to the grisly discovery out on the eastern shoreline had nothing to do with Darla. Or Mason. Or anyone they knew.

Or so Darla thought.

CHAPTER 24

"Last time you were here, we talked about someplace deep down, do you remember?"

"Yes. Holy Orders." She remembered. It was all she'd thought about the intervening week.

"Do you remember we compared a marriage to an apple tree. You tend the tree to help it grow and flourish, like you tend your marriage."

"And," she added, "in the absence of caretakers, God tends a marriage. And it didn't make sense to me then. It still doesn't."

"What if we change the metaphor? Say, instead of an apple tree, your marriage is a house."

"Something not found in nature?" She was being obstinate, but there had to be a bottom to this. She had to find it, too. If not for getting clear answers, then why were they in a marriage retreat? What was there to save?

"Well, think of this. A house is built with wood and mortar, steel. Natural elements."

"And the things inside of it?"

He smiled. "Are what make it a home. God gives us the basics. He gives us the seeds and the soil, the rain and the wind."

"And the lumber and the manpower." She nodded slowly. Though his sermon was still questionably ambiguous, she felt the inkling of appreciation. If not for the logic in his lecture, then the heart.

"God gave us enough to keep us safe and get started. The rest is up to us. Whether our home-grown apple trees flourish, or whether they wither away."

"Whether our homes are filled with happiness and love." For the first time in any of their sessions— either the ones with her husband or the private ones —she got choked up. Tears welled in her eyes. Her heart raced in her chest. Sobs built up in her throat.

He looked at her with an expression of compassion and patience. "Is yours? Is your house a home?"

She considered this a moment. "What if I don't want it to be?"

CHAPTER 25—TATUM

Tatum had a slew of intakes come in on Friday. She was barely prepared. First, a mama cat and her litter of nine—*nine!* Then, a pair of strays ferried in on a private boat by Kate Hannigan. Kate had found them begging for paltry scraps at the all-but-barren marina. They'd gotten into some fisherman's bucket of fish—fresh from a day of ice-fishing farther north. The fisherman was ready to shoot the dogs on sight, but Kate intervened and had her partner drive them out to Tatum.

It didn't stop there. After lunch, a goat was tied off to Tatum's mailbox. She had no idea where the poor thing had come from or what, really, to do with it. She could scarcely tell if it was a boy goat or a girl goat, but she knew that all living things needed shelter, food, drink, and love. And Tatum had those things to give. So, she gave them all.

It took her the better half of the morning brushing out the dogs and goat and trying to wipe the cat and kittens down with warm wet cloths. Then food and drink. Then pens. The cats got the cat room that was in the back of the farmhouse. The goat got the third stall of the barn. The dogs had the run, with access to a warm cove that spilled into the mudroom of the house.

Once everyone was settled, Tatum scrounged for her phone. She sent off a text to Rip, who'd stayed on the mainland that day, negotiating a new contract with Mr. Rutherford and team. From Tatum's understanding, they'd have to amend the current contract with a majority board approval. Without board approval, the contract would go into breach, and technically, lawsuits could follow. No one involved wanted to litigate the already tetchy situation. It was a lose-lose. Rutherford's mission and vision and opening plans were in limbo. Rip's ability to close out the project was, too.

Of course, Rip *did* kind of have reason to be pleased with the delay. If he cared at all for the Sageberry sisters, then he cared for St. Mary's. And if he cared for St. Mary's, he cared for the enrollment conundrum. But Rip was a professional through and through. He'd made no attempts to deliberately stall the project. It was nature that had taken her course. Nature and, potentially, a murderer.

Tatum finished her text message. *Don't forget dinner at the boardwalk tonight!* Afterward, she was hoping Rip would stay for a family game night. Then maybe they'd go for a stroll along the lakeshore, snuggled in layers, watching their breath puff as they each confessed their surprising and yet undying love, one for the other.

I'll be there <3

The heart emoji was a first, and Tatum's own real heart fluttered at the sight of it. She wanted to send back one thousand hearts. But she didn't. Instead, she settled for a winking face. It felt a little more provocative. A little more risqué. A little more *Tatum*.

After, Tatum cracked open her laptop and went in the backdoor to her website to make updates on the new tenants. From there she moved to her social media pages, updating as she went. At last, she moved to the local online groups where she'd blast out a post that the weekend was the perfect time to welcome a new family member into the home!

It was then, when she landed on Heirloom

Island Online Community of Neighbors that she read a post so shocking she had to read it twice.

A third time.

ISLAND REMAINS ID'D! The poster announced in all capital letters. In true social-media form, however, the original poster hadn't said to whom the body had belonged. Instead, they left it vague so as to rustle up drama and conflict and all the things the best viral posts were made of.

Tatum read down through the dozens of comments. Many were just asking *Who is it???* Others threw up what were no doubt meant to be hilarious guesses. None were funny, though. Not even D.B. Cooper.

In the mix were a few more serious guesses. At least, Tatum took them to be such. Names she didn't know of people whose prayers had been answered in all the wrong ways. Her heart hurt for them. The mother from the mainland whose teen daughter had run away decades before. The wife of the husband who left for work one day and never came back. The once-a-child-now-an-adult who never knew her bio-mom, but who knew the woman had once visited Heirloom Island for a vacation. Heartbreaking, all of them.

But there was one name that came up again and

again. Various commenters had chimed in either guessing it or confirming it, apparently. Several noted that they had it on good authority it was definitely her. This name was no less heartbreaking to Tatum, but it was all the more familiar.

And, all the more worrisome.

Tatum chewed her bottom lip until it nearly bled. Then, she called her sister.

CHAPTER 26—CADENCE

Cadence smoothed her hands down her thighs for the umpteenth time. Kirk had brought her water. Nothing more, but nothing less, either.

Now they were staring awkwardly at one another again. She opted for an observation. Wasn't that a great way to start a conversation, anyhow? Observing and reporting? It worked for police, at least. She pointed at a beautiful stained glass window. Depicted within it, Mother Mary holding the Baby Jesus. "Are you Catholic?"

He looked surprised at the question. "Me?" A slight adjustment to his glasses and then a short cough into his fist. Everything he did seemed pat and neat and quick. "Yes. Well, I was born Catholic.

I've not been great about going to Mass." Then he looked at her more meaningfully. "Assuming you're a woman of faith, is that important to you? Is it something you want to talk about?"

Cadence thought his phrasing funny, but she reminded herself he was uncomfortable with this— whatever it was. Platonic or not, men could be uneasy in the company of women. Hendrik had once told Cadence that, and she liked the idea of it. It gave her a small sense of power. A boost to her confidence, even. "Well, as a matter of fact, yes. I am Catholic, and it's a big part of my life. I go to church. I take Communion. Confession once or twice a year. More if necessary." She laughed nervously. The admission came out like a flirty little one-liner, though she hadn't meant it to. "Not that I'm ever a bad—" Ugh! She rolled her eyes and laughed again. "I'm sorry. That's silly."

He held up an apologetic hand. "No, no. You can talk about it, if you wish?"

"Not really." She admired the stained glass a beat longer. When he didn't go on to talk more about his Catholic upbringing or how the home came to be adorned so beautifully by the Blessed Mother, Cadence tried to push ahead. "Were you living here when the old monastery was functioning?" It was a question she'd wanted to ask a local. Cadence had only just arrived at the island a couple of years before the place closed down. She didn't know much about it, and any seeds of information she might gain from locals regarding the site of the former monastery or future school might benefit her— personally and professionally. Still, she kept her tone light and conversational, as opposed to journal- istic or voyeuristic, even.

"Yes, sure. Sure." He stretched slightly back and looked off through the front window toward the lake. He had no view of the construction site from that vantage point, but it wasn't too far away from his house there on the northeast corner of Heirloom. Then his eyebrows furrowed. "How about you?" Kirk crossed one leg over the other then hooked his hands around the top knee, giving her an open, sensitive look.

"Just a bit," she answered. "It closed up not long after I moved here."

"And what brought you to Heirloom in the first place?" Now they were rolling, even if he'd success- fully led her away from the monastery locale.

She smiled fondly. "St. Mary's. I got the job there,

and lived in one of the little dorm rooms they reserve for teachers. It was a special time. My first job. A new town. An *island*, at that." A thought occurred to her. "I suppose we might have even run into each other back then and not have known it!"

He shook his head, though. "Possibly, but I doubt it. I left after high school. It's only this winter that I've returned to live here."

Cadence didn't bother to note the year she'd moved there. It'd only serve to age her, and with Kirk, she didn't really feel like talking about age. It had dominated her last romantic relationship. *Not* that this was anything romantic. Of course, it wasn't. He was a new friend. Nothing more.

She fell quiet a moment, and Kirk shifted again in his seat. "Cadence, why don't we talk about what's going on with you." Another odd phrasing.

"Oh. Okay." She blinked fast a few times. Was this it? Was this him asking if she was hitting the dating scene? If she'd effectively mourned Hendrik's death and moved on? Because if he was, she hadn't. Not all the way. She played it cool. "Well, Tatum has the shelter up and running. I think that's going well. It'll be a slow process. I know she's anxious to mone-tize it—maybe that's not the right word. She's anxious to fund it. A few grants are coming in, but they are pretty limited in scope. The more attention she can drive in, the better, of course." Cadence gave her head a nod. "But, yes. She's doing really well for herself. Plus, Rip. Do you know Rip?"

Kirk nodded again.

"Oh, right. You know all the Van Dams, I suppose. Well, I think the two are an item. Nothing official, of course. Just the beginning. It's exciting, those early days. Isn't it?" She looked at him, but she hadn't meant to.

Kirk looked away fast and cleared his throat. His nervousness appeared to transform into something else. Was he aggravated? Put off?

Cadence felt embarrassed, and so she moved on to Darla. "And Darla is becoming a mother. The most important thing in the world." Cadence didn't tamp down on the wistfulness she felt at making such a bold claim. It came out in her voice, in her face. She could feel herself light up from the inside out when she talked about motherhood. Cadence would never be a mother. Not like Darla, at least. She'd been a stepmother, and that had been good enough, probably. But Cadence wouldn't have her own children. She was past that now. Maybe that was why she was feeling so content back at the school. Maybe that was also why she was so uncomfortable about what was going on with the construction site. The discovery. The new school.

"You say that being a mother is the most important thing in the world," Kirk said, by way of an oddly echoing repetition of her words. Cadence felt like something was off.

"Yes?" she asked, looking around for a candid camera crew or something of the sort.

"I just wonder why is all." He said this so simply, that she felt silly for being offended. It made sense that he'd ask after her thoughts about motherhood. She's the one who brought it up, for one. And for two, if, like Cadence suspected, Kirk Sanders was even the tiniest bit interested romantically—which she'd shut down anyway—he'd probably want to know. Did Cadence wish to have her own children one day? Was that important to *her*?

"Oh, well." She sighed lightly and gave it a thought. "I suppose it stems from my religious and spiritual beliefs. The nuclear family and the church family and everything about the family. You know? It's innate that we sort of seek that model of life out."

"What about those monks from the monastery?" Kirk's question settled Cadence. They were having a two-way conversation, stilted at times, though it may be.

"And nuns, too. A different calling. A blessed calling. They marry the Church. Jesus Christ. God. And their children exist, sure. Just in a different way. For a monk, his children are his parishioners. And a nun, the children she serves." Cadence shrugged. "That's my understanding of it all, at least."

"What about you?" Kirk asked. "You don't have biological children. And for that matter, what about any woman who neither has biological children nor wishes to join the Convent?"

Academic, this conversation. Cadence liked it. She didn't have all the answers, which is why she enjoyed their back-and-forth. It was more as though she was coming to an understanding with Kirk. She decided to answer by way of a question of her own. "So, you disagree? We aren't naturally disposed to long for families?"

He adjusted his glasses and looked briefly at his lap before returning her gaze. "Quite the contrary. It's biological, to be sure. I just wonder how *you* feel, Cadence. I wonder if part of your grief over losing Hendrik is also the grief of children that could have been?" He gave her a harder stare now, and it shook Cadence loose from her delusion.

She stood abruptly. "This is a *therapy* session?"

Kirk joined her. "Well, yes."

"I quit therapy. I thought I told you that! I thought this was tea and lunch. And—a friendly thing. Not *therapy*." She was backing up through his living room now, moving slowly, shocked and unmoored and horrified to have been made such a fool in front of Kirk Sanders. *Dr.* Sanders.

"Cadence, wait." He was following her, his hands raised to slow her down, his steps slow to match hers.

"I feel like an idiot. I thought we were friends. I thought—"

"I thought you booked this for therapy," he objected. The tension started to break, but by then, they were at his door. Cadence was pulling on her coat and scarf. Kirk was red in the face. His hands had moved down deep in his pockets. He looked younger. He looked as foolish-feeling as Cadence was. "Cadence, I'm terribly sorry."

"Me, too. I thought this—" she waved a hand between them, but the gesture came out all wrong.

"You thought there was something...?" he searched for the words to finish her sentence.

"No," Cadence said sharply. "I didn't think there was *something*." She glowered at him, but her expression softened when she saw he was hurt by the harshness of her tone. "Why? Did *you*?"

Cadence watched as Kirk's Adam's apple bobbed up and down. He adjusted his glasses then put his hand back into his pocket. "I'm your therapist. That's why I invited you here today. For a session." His jaw was set.

And Cadence was out the door.

CHAPTER 27—CADENCE

Her feelings hurt and raw from humiliation, Cadence pulled her car over to the side of the road once she was a mile from his house and farther inland. Patches of snow peppered the ground there. Remnants of a winter that had only just begun.

Cadence considered this. The fact that winter didn't end with the New Year like it should have. As a child growing up, and even as a stepmother to the girls, it always felt as though Christmas were the peak of the cold season. Christmas day snow, and perhaps dregs of the white stuff through New Year's Eve...then *bam*. A new year, a warm spell. Right? The New Year should bring with it blasts of the stuff—of warm sun and melting ice and happiness.

But it never did. Christmas and then into New

Year's Day was only ever the beginning of the pain of ice and snow. And even when it didn't snow or when a warm day poked its head through the clouds, you could be sure Winter wasn't done with you yet.

Cadence didn't stay there, on the side of the road, and cry. She didn't snivel. She accepted it. She accepted she'd made a grave error. Assuming a man, or even a *person*, would invite her for tea and lunch had been nothing short of silly. And why had she been so readily and so easily mixed up? Now, *that*, was unlike Cadence. Sure-footed and even-keeled ruled the day, and Cadence was nothing if not a collected woman. To miss the message and get everything wrong—how embarrassing. How utterly embarrassing.

But something good had come. Something good had come from her brief, misguided time on Kirk Sanders' sofa.

She'd had a breakthrough.

And it was entirely thanks to him.

CHAPTER 28

It was their last marital session, and she was unsatisfied. More so than when she'd begun this whole thing.

The last time she'd spoken with Brother, she'd asked him the one question that had gotten them there, in marriage counseling:

What if I don't want to make my house a home?

He hadn't answered, but she suspected this wasn't for lack of an answer. Rather, he'd told her to think about it. She'd left without telling him that all she did was think about it. About how she was a bad wife and a bad mother and a bad person because of the first two things.

Now, she and her husband were back, and the answer to her question felt more elusive than ever.

"Let's begin with a prayer," Brother said. He seemed colder that day. More distant than ever. Like he'd already mentally graduated them.

They moved through the motions. Prayer. Sharing time. Questions from him. Nothing was new. Everything was review.

Tell me about your date this week, directed Brother.

We saw a movie in Birch Harbor. Supposed to be a romantic comedy, but it wasn't all that funny, replied her husband.

I agree. And she did. It was funny, the things you agreed about when you were on the cusp of the end times.

And that's just where they were, too. On that last day of their retreat, the couple was at the end.

But only one of them knew it.

CHAPTER 29—DARLA

Darla's phone rang at last. She looked at the screen then up at the others.

The dining room table was a hodgepodge of important people. Mason sat near her, his face placid. Rip sat on the far side of Mason. His expression was harder to read. More troubled, maybe.

Beyond Rip, Tatum held a fussy Shep. Gabe was asleep in the playpen in the living room, and it was the first time, Darla was pretty certain, that they weren't napping at the exact same hour. It felt like a bad omen. Tatum's focus was on shushing the baby.

It was the person across from Tatum who gave Darla the most urgent look.

Faye, who'd taken a boat from the mainland to

join them, frowned deeply at Darla then looked more pointedly at the phone.

Mila was on the way, too. They couldn't yet get in touch with Lotte.

"Well?" Faye pressed. "Is it her?"

Darla nodded.

It was Cadence. Finally. After an hour of trying to get in touch with her. An hour of scrambling people together at the boardwalk house. An hour of wondering where in the world Cadence was—because she'd only mentioned lunch with a friend, and no one knew who the friend was or where the lunch would be—she was calling them back.

"Cadence?" Darla answered, almost nervous that someone else had Cadence's phone. Maybe it wasn't her. Maybe this big drama was about to grow degrees bigger.

But Cadence's voice returned the greeting warmly. "Darla, oh my goodness. I have to tell you what just happened. It's been a crazy day. I—"

"Cadence, where are you? Where have you been?"

"That lunch I was supposed to have—it's, well it's embarrassing really. I'll explain that later, but I want to tell you what I realized. Yes, Darla. I had a realization, and I'm just about to burst from it."

"Cadence, wait, I need to actually tell you—"

"Darla, I've had a breakthrough."

"What?" Darla looked at the others who were growing obviously impatient and curious with her. She indicated to them to wait a moment, and she listened to whatever it was Cadence had to say.

"I'm coming home. I'll tell you everything when I'm there, but I had to get this out."

"Get what out?"

"Children, Darla. It's all about children. Children and Hendrik and the girls."

"The girls as in—?" Darla looked around the table at the others who sat rapt. Even Shep had stopped fussing and was watching his mom from his aunt's arms.

"The *girls*. Faye, Lotte, and Mila."

"Right. The girls."

"Darla, I'll never *really* get over Hendrik, you know? He was the love of my life. But I think I can move on from his death. I think I figured it out."

"That's great, Cadence." Darla waited for another bomb to drop. A bigger one than had an hour earlier.

"I never had my own children. I always wanted to, but I never did. And as much love as I could give the girls, and as much love as they gave me—there was always a shadow looming. You know?"

"A shadow?" Darla was growing more fretful now. Where was this going? And why did it feel like Cadence was about to confess something big.

"Katarina," Cadence answered. "Katarina. The girls' mother. Her absence all these years was a shadow. When would she come back? How? What would it mean to our family if she did? Honestly, Darla, I dreaded it. I dreaded that she'd come back.

She was saying way too much. "Cadence, be quiet," Darla spat urgently. "Don't say another word."

"What?"

Darla swallowed and replied, "Just get home."

CHAPTER 30—TATUM

Baby Shep was falling asleep in Tatum's arms, and so she dare not move. None of them dared to move. The news of the identification of the remains had sent shockwaves through the island and through the Sageberrys and their friends. Everyone was on alert. The whole of it felt surreal.

Even Tatum, who normally flew under the radar of other people's dramas, was now affected. The identity of the woman could change everything she'd come to enjoy. It could change everything stable in Tatum's life and in her sisters'. And especially with the oddness in Darla's face at talking to Cadence—as if there were much, *much* more to this story.

Beneath the table, Rip rested his hand on

Tatum's thigh. It was meant as a gesture of confidence and affection, but it made Tatum even more nervous. Like he might be saying, *Don't worry about this. It'll all blow over.*

The problem was it would not blow over. The investigation at the construction site would heat back up. The new build would go on hold. Rip would have no other reason to come to Heirloom other than Tatum, and what if she wasn't enough of a reason to begin with? What if she was a footnote on Rip's professional career? She didn't think she was, but you never knew. And they still hadn't really talked about things.

Cadence was expected in a matter of moments, which was why the knock at the front door startled all of them. Gabe woke up in his playpen and started to cry. Darla rushed to him, and Tatum joined her at the sofa, Shep now peacefully asleep in her arms.

While the two sisters settled into the sofa with the babies, Rip took it upon himself to answer the door. Mason followed him. They acted something like sentries or security for Darla and Tatum, and this was greatly appreciated. Not that the women needed men in their lives, but they needed, well, *help*. In some way, shape, or form. And here it was—the help. In the form of Rip, the man Tatum thought she was falling for. And in the form of Mason, the man who clearly had a crush on Darla but for whom no feelings were yet returned.

They spoke in low tones to an unseen person, and so Tatum leaned over to Darla. "Why did Mason come?" She hadn't had a chance to ask Darla this.

"He came with Rip. What are you talking about?" Darla whispered back.

"I mean, why did he come, though?"

Darla gave her a look. "Why did Rip come?"

"Because it's his business. It's his build."

"Oh, so he didn't come for you?"

Now it was Tatum's turn to give her sister a look. "Are you saying Mason came for *you*?"

Darla turned flustered. "No. I'm saying he came for *us*. And anyway, he's the one who told me about all of this, remember? So, I guess that makes it his business, too."

Tatum smirked. Mason had nothing to do with the remains, with the building site, or with Cadence or Tatum. Her mind flickered back to their last conversation, and she whispered again to Darla, "Is he here trying to recruit you, then?" Maybe Mason was desperate. Maybe he was so desperate to help his school hire a new teacher that he was here under false pretenses. Tatum knew this was ridiculous, of course. But she also knew that Darla did *not* know Mason's school was hiring a teacher.

"What?" Darla hissed, but their time was up. Mason and Rip were inviting a pair of men dressed in trench coats and wearing black scarves. They looked exactly how you'd expect a pair of detectives to look.

CHAPTER 31

The husband left the bare, wooden room first, almost as if to give her and Brother a private moment.

She waited until there was silence beyond the room.

"Thanks for everything you've done for us."

"It's what you've done for you," he replied.

She sucked her lips between her teeth and waited a beat. "You know, I thought this would go somewhere else." She passed her hand between the two of them, suggestively but not sexually, if that was possible. With friars, it was.

He gave her a funny look, but it fell away just as she was about to retract her statement. He said, "It still can."

She was tingling with anticipation, but not the anticipation of a crush or the chance of a new love. She was tingling with anticipation for a fresh start a different life. The path she should have taken had she ever bothered to read that boring Robert Frost poem that seemed to be pushed down every teenager's throat since the old poet had died and gone and made himself posthumously famous.

"It can't, though." Obligation outweighed everything. Ultimately, she was a mother before she could ever be anything else.

"Why not?" He looked at her with clear eyes. Earnest, serious, daring eyes, as if he might say, "It's time. It's time for you to live the life you might have. You can have it all, even with our faith, you can have it all."

But she knew better. "My kids. I can't leave them." She sniffed. "I won't leave them."

"But you'd leave him."

She snorted. "It's a package deal. You haven't seen the lengths to which he'll go to keep me."

The friar looked at her with great surprise, as though he'd never once considered just how bad things were. He looked at her, she thought, as if this morsel of information might have changed everything. If only she'd shared it much, much earlier.

But it wasn't her husband's control that she wanted out of. It was the control of any man or person. What she wanted more than marriage was the peace that she hadn't experienced in a decade or more. The kind of peace, she figured, that this kindly faced, simple monk knew. The peace of someone who'd taken a dangerous, risky commitment and made it their life.

If only women could be monks. She'd just stay there.

As though he read her mind, Brother said, "One day, when your children are grown, you can return here. I know several places for you, and I can help you transition."

"I can't just leave my marriage," she reiterated.

"You can have an annulment. I can help. You can do that sooner than later, even." His tone dropped low. "If you are in danger, you need to say that now. We have resources. We can help you."

"Oh yeah?" she laughed, mirthless at this late advice. Too late.

"There's an annex on the south side of our monastery, like a small house. Some of the Brothers call it a little priory. It's where we host our Sisters when they join us for the Advent season, as special guests. They come other times, too. We often have one or two there, although right now, it's empty."

"What's there?"

"We have beds, a bathroom, and a kitchenette. It's a bit like a dormitory."

"So, someone could live there. Like, a house?"

He cracked a smile. "Or, if you prefer, it could be a *home*."

She did not return the smile. "Not long-term."

"God gives us the resources. We decide what to do with them."

"I'll be fine." She sucked down all the emotion that was festering. "I'll figure it out."

"If you do ever need a place to come, our doors are open, both here in the monastery and in our little shelter house."

"Shelter house? Don't you mean *priory home*?"

He gave her one last sad look. It wouldn't be the final time she spoke to him, but it would be the last time she saw him, though she didn't know it then. She tried to smile in return, but instead, found herself falling into his arms, into a warm, safe hug. A brotherly hug. One of promise and hope and the possibility that one day she would return to the monastery or the little house at its corner, reserved for women who helped other women and women who needed help, too.

Suddenly, behind them and their embrace, the door swung open.

Standing in the doorframe, his face beet red, was her husband.

The singular, formidable Hendrik Van Dam.

CHAPTER 32—CADENCE

Cadence was floating on Cloud 9. Disappointment over her faulty expectations about the luncheon with Kirk couldn't seep into her newfound hope. She couldn't wait to get home and talk to her sisters about it. She felt like she'd gained a new set of wings and was ready to take off.

Heck, maybe she'd even keep up the therapy sessions after all. Although, now it'd be pretty awkward if she did.

A light snowfall began to descend as she turned off the main road and into her drive along the boardwalk. Winter was back.

And so too were the police cars from earlier in the week.

Cadence cocked her head as she parked the car.

Hm. Along with the police cars, Tatum's truck and the work truck Rip used while he was working on Heirloom.

Her brow furrowed further. Was this about the thing with Rutherford? Had he pressed some sort of charge against Rip and Tatum or something?

Or was it—

Cadence felt her breath catch in her throat. No. She'd been paranoid. There was no way her very worst dream was about to come true. Not now. Not after she'd pretty much laid the whole question to rest.

She left her car and hurried through the cold, wet flakes and to her own door. Before she could even turn the knob, it opened.

On the other side, stood Faye, her eyes red-rimmed.

It was even worse than Cadence thought.

Nobody had said anything to Cadence when she first walked in. Not Faye or Tatum or Darla. Not Rip or Mason. Not the two obvious detectives, either. They acted like they'd been waiting for Cadence, in fact. They acted like it was she who was to receive whatever news they had. And Faye's presence suggested the whole thing actually had quite little, if anything, to do with Tatum.

So, suffice it to say, everyone was suitably tense once Cadence followed the group to the living room. Most of them found a seat on a sofa or armchair. The two detectives stood uncomfortably in front of Cadence's fireplace.

Cadence clasped her hands in her lap and stole another glance at Faye, who sat next her and now put in great effort to stop what must have been another wave of tears. She sniffled uncontrollably. Cadence grabbed her hand and squeezed it, sourcing strength from her eldest stepdaughter. The one who was hardest to win over. The quiet one. The writer.

"What is all this about?" she looked at Faye then at her own sisters, awaiting any morsel of an explanation. Several of the group cleared their throats. Gazes slid away. Faye's sniffles went quiet.

At last, Cadence looked at the officers. "Is this about the remains?" she knew, instinctively, that it was. They, however, seemed surprised.

"It is. Yes." A frown tugged down the older detective's features. Not one of suspicion, but one, just the same, of curiosity. "We've positively identified them."

At this, Cadence lost all control. She burst into tears that had been hovering just at the surface for the past week. Maybe longer. Maybe the tears had started the night Kirk Sanders spilled the beans on the new charter school.

As she wept into balled up fists, Tatum and Darla left their place on the sofa to surround her and wrap her in their arms. "Cadence, shh," Darla whispered.

Tatum kept her voice low and soft, too. "Why are you crying?"

"There's no way she's part of this, officers," Mason protested.

"Part of it?" Cadence rubbed her face and looked up. "Of course I'm part of it!" she wailed through her fists. "I'm the *cause* of it!"

As if there weren't enough confusion as it was, the front door burst open and in through it fell none other than Dr. Kirk Sanders, himself.

"Kirk?" Cadence's face twisted up.

"Kirk." Rip strode to him hurriedly. "What's up, man?"

"I just read the news. The remains. Cadence—I worried she'd be—" He looked worried, too Actually, he looked panicked. His face was stretched out at odd angles, and his sweater bunched and twisted like he'd taken it off then pulled it back on in a hurry. "Are you okay?" Kirk was speaking now to Cadence, directly, like no one else in the room existed.

Why he would care, she wasn't sure. Instead of answering him, Cadence, whose face was only just now drying from her own panic, turned to the others. "He's my therapist. I guess."

"I'm your friend, too," Kirk added. This bolstered Cadence and she wiped the last tear from her face.

"Well, thank you."

"Cadence," the older detective said. "Can we have a private word with you regarding this?" He gestured toward the office, which was Tatum's now-former bedroom.

Cadence stood, bravely, and smoothed her blouse. "Of course."

Before she went, Darla grabbed her arm. "You did this, Cade?"

"Did what?" Cadence looked into her sister's wild expression, now unsure exactly what was going on. "We're talking about the body, right. The school?"

"What do you mean we're talking about the school?" Darla hissed back, stealing a glance at the detectives who now moved into the office. "This has nothing to do with the school."

"It has to do with the school. It's not going to open is it? The new charter school? And it's because of me. I've advocated against it. In my heart and in reality. I wrote a letter to the paper, Darla." Cadence looked down, ashamed. "I made it clear I didn't want the new school built, and now look. A dead body is found there, and so the school won't be built."

"It's not about the school," Darla repeated, her teeth gritted. "It's the remains. You don't know? You really don't?" She was frowning hard at Cadence.

Faye came up behind Darla now, and Tatum joined them.

The younger detective cleared his throat at the door to the office. "Ms. Van Dam?"

"Just a minute, Detective." Cadence looked back at her sisters and at Faye. She started to ask *what? What is it I don't know?*

But before she could, the front door burst open for a second time that evening. In the doorway, a bedraggled girl.

Mila.

Her face was red from the cold and her eyes wet with tears or snow—it was hard to tell. "Is it really her?" Mila asked.

"Is what really who?" Cadence demanded, now falling back a step from Darla and Faye and Tatum and taking in the room anew, as if it were foreign territory. Because it was. And whatever secret she'd just entered into was not what she thought. The drama here was not that Cadence wished the new school ill. It was something else.

Something far more personal to the Sageberrys.

And the Van Dams.

Cadence's throat went dry as she croaked again. "Who did they find at the construction site? Whose body was that?"

Faye opened her arms as Mila rushed into them. They were in their own world, the two young sisters.

Darla took Cadence's elbow. "Cadence, it was *her.*"

"No," Cadence whispered. "How can it be?"

Tatum nodded miserably. "It's *her.*"

Of course. It made sense. Who else did they know who'd gone missing so many years back that what was left of the person was all but dust?

Darla squeezed Cadence who'd started crying all over again. She murmured the damning confirmation into Cadence's ear. "It's Katarina."

Katarina Van Dam.

Hendrik's first wife.

The girls' mother.

CHAPTER 33—DARLA

The funeral for Katarina Sanders-Van Dam was a quiet affair. Not that funerals were generally noisy. But this one, especially, proved somber. Almost hollow, even. Yet, despite how quiet an affair it was, it was bizarrely well attended.

Darla and Tatum had taken it upon themselves to coordinate things. After all, there was nowhere else, truly, to have expansive events on Heirloom Island. The boardwalk house that once was Cadence's venue dream was the only place left, truly. And anyway, it was sitting open. No tenants. No bookings.

Just the funeral.

It made sense.

During the planning phase, the previous weekend, Cadence even suggested that this be the final event ever to be held at the house. She'd like to see it turned into something else entirely, once this dark business was finally closed.

Darla had protested, but only gently. *I might be able to turn a profit, Cadence.* It was useless. Cadence had declared that she loved Darla so much, that she knew Darla shouldn't do something that wasn't in her blood, like teaching was.

And Cadence had been right.

So, the funeral would be it. Katarina's remains had been reduced to ashes and stowed in a gorgeous Dutch-made urn shipped special order from abroad. She wouldn't need a casket. All she needed was to be respectfully laid to rest.

"Hey." Mason sidled up next to Darla at the bar they'd set up. March on the island could be just as frigid as January, maybe even more so. As such, everyone was buttoned up in heavy sweaters and coats and long pants. Scarves and overcoats had been carefully stored in the parlor at the front of the house, where Tatum had thought to bring in a menagerie of old coat racks and a couple of wobbly desks left behind in her farmhouse. Tatum was good at things like that, and they'd had the time to dedicate to the task that was burying the victim of foul play.

Darla smiled at him and tipped her drink, a wine. She couldn't remember the last time she'd had wine. Not that this was celebratory, but there was something to be said for everything that had coalesced over the past several months. From her decision to stay home, of the discovery to the body and news that it was Katarina Van Dam, who'd somehow wound up between two old footers of a flower bed. And then of course the shared decision among the sisters that the events business and venue was a nonstarter. Cadence had school. Tatum had the shelter. And Darla had—the boys. And she'd have to find another income stream somehow, assuming she wanted to. Cadence was firm in her promise that she could help Darla for as long as Darla needed. It was just the two of them there, in the boardwalk house, not counting the boys whose needs were surprisingly minimal. Diapers and wipes. Formula. And otherwise, Darla made do with hand-me-downs from the local mothers' group she'd joined. She wasn't too concerned with being a fancy mom. Just a good one.

"Hi."

Mason took a long drink from his brandy,

savoring it, maybe. Or thinking about what he was going to say next, maybe. "This is sad."

"Yeah. The girls are upset. More so than I'd have imagined."

"What do you mean?"

"They weren't close to their mom. At least, that's what Cadence told us. She said when she married Hendrik, he'd done his job well."

Mason cringed. The truth of what had happened had spread like wildfire across their crook of Michigan. "Did Cadence have a similar experience?"

"What, you mean during their marriage?"

"Yeah, sure. How can a guy go that far with one wife and treat the next like nothing ever happened?"

Tatum and Cadence walked up to them at that moment, each reaching for a fresh glass of wine.

Mason cleared his throat and looked uneasily at Darla.

Darla nodded toward the stairs. "The boys are upstairs with Mila. I should go take over so she can come down." The arrangement was to take the boys in shifts. They'd give the girls a good distraction and Darla, Tatum, and Cadence each a break throughout the funeral.

"I can help." Mason followed her.

CHAPTER 34—TATUM

"Here." Tatum passed a drink to Cadence, who'd been on the verge of hyperventilating. "Take this, then go up after Darla. Take a break. You deserve it."

Cadence swigged the wine and nodded. "Yeah. Okay."

She started for the stairs, and Tatum watched her go, but before Cadence even made it to the first step, she was interceded. It was him.

The one who'd conferred with the police. Who'd told them everything. Who'd all but singlehandedly solved the mystery of Katarina Van Dam—where she'd gone and why.

Dr. Kirk Sanders.

Rip appeared, however, blocking Tatum's view

and her urge to call him off. Cadence couldn't take it. "Hey."

Tatum frowned and leaned left to see after Cadence and Kirk, but Rip leaned with her. "Hey," he repeated. "It's okay."

She lifted a hand uselessly, "She won't want to talk to him."

"Give him a chance. Kirk's a good guy, Tate." He rubbed her arm then leaned in to kiss her on the cheek. "What does he have to say to her?" Tatum caught a view of Kirk and Cadence leaving the bottom of the staircase and winding out past the foyer and slipping through the front door.

"I should really go after."

"Tatum, can we talk?" Rip ran a hand up the back of his neck. He looked nervous. Shy and bashful, and all of Tatum's doubts that Rip was wrong washed away.

"Talk? Of course."

CHAPTER 35

Rip steered Tatum outside, where it was chilly but not too cold. Rip apologized.

"I'm sorry it's cold out here, and we're at a funeral, which is...bad timing." He rubbed his hands together then rubbed her arms up and down as if to warm her. But a warm feeling was already pooling inside of Tatum.

"Bad timing?" Her ears pricked.

"Tatum, I know how I feel about you, and I think I know how you feel about me." He hesitated and frowned. "Well, how *do* you feel about me?"

"Honestly?"

He nodded, eager.

"I like you, like, a lot, Rip. Like, a weird amount. Like, I don't know if I've ever liked someone as much as I like you. Sometimes I think..." she swallowed and blinked fast. It was ridiculous, what she wanted to say. So ridiculous that she really shouldn't say it.

But he did. "Tatum, I'm falling in love with you."

Without thinking about it, she laced her fingers into his and they leaned into each other, their gazes locked. "I'm falling in love with you, too, I think."

"So, what do we do about this?"

"Well, you could...be my boyfriend? Maybe?"

"Actually, I was thinking of something a little... more dramatic."

She froze up as Rip pulled something out of his pocket. It couldn't be. They weren't even a couple, not officially. There was no way this was happening. Tatum did quick math in her head. She'd met Rip, like, a year earlier. Well, she'd met him way earlier than that, but they actually met and started talking a year earlier. Not even! It was March back then, and then after that it wasn't until late summer they, like, *really* started talking, and then the dates didn't start until after that, and why hadn't he ever asked her to be exclusive? And wasn't that the normal order of events? Her heart raced, and her breath turned short. He was on one knee now. A velvet box in his hand. His face lifted to hers, worry streaked over it, probably matching her own expression.

Tatum knew she had only one option. She had to do the thing that had gotten her by in life. She'd never relied on logic or math or sensibility to be happy, and look where that had gotten her. It had gotten her her life's dream. An animal shelter. And... even more than that, it had gotten her together with this guy who was so lovable and so kind that you couldn't help but adore him and before Rip even said a single word, Tatum fell to her knees and gripped his face with her hands and rushed to say, loudly and clearly, "I want to marry you."

CHAPTER 36—CADENCE

The entirety of the events of the past few months had worn her out. And they'd required strength Cadence didn't know she had.

What was the worst about it all, was how she'd only just found a way to move on from Hendrik. She'd only just managed to accept that she could love him even after his death, but she could find new love and new happiness, too.

Then the bomb was dropped.

Kirk found out via the news that the remains at the monastery belonged to Katarina. Apparently, he came forward about having once been at the monastery.

The details were worse than Cadence could have

imagined. The details still felt surreal to her, and in the past three months she'd done her best to keep her head down and teach and focus on her job and her sisters and her nephews. The thoughts swished around inside of her. Cadence was mired in the grisly details of how her deceased husband, his deceased first wife, and Cadence's own current friend and therapist were all so tragically connected. It was much for her to swallow.

But now the funeral was here, and Cadence knew that with funerals, came honesty. People revealed their true selves and their inner truths at funerals, almost like the funeral was less a celebration and memorial to the deceased and more of a confession for the living.

"Cadence, please," Kirk begged her at the stairs. "Can we talk?"

She'd ignored his calls and texts and, indeed, the salacious media coverage surrounding him. "I'd like a chance to explain myself to you."

"Why? It's not like—I mean, I left your practice. You realize that, don't you?"

He gripped her elbow, lightly but with intention. "Can we talk somewhere else?"

She looked past him to see Tatum and Rip watching. "Follow me."

They left through the front door and got comfortable in her car, the heat on and quiet pop music playing low.

"Okay." Cadence looked straight ahead at her house. It was beautiful, the home. But lately, it hadn't much felt like it belonged to her. It felt much more like a house that once belonged to a different family. Not hers. It occurred to her now, with this unusual moment to reflect on the house from the outside, the very outside, what similarities the three boardwalk houses held. Each was different, but the style was there. The Van Dam style. Broad and tall, like a monument to God himself.

All three had columns shooting up from them, which belied the religious tone, referencing instead some degree of the Federalist architecture from so many years before. Or, even more than that, the Roman empire.

And that was Hendrik, really. An emperor, of his own family and of the island at large. Heirloom Island. An inheritance passed down from those first families, with all their Catholic fortitude and hope and defiance of whatever problems affected them on the mainland. Those families took a more dangerous road. Actually, they hardly took a road, instead preferring the soft waves of Lake Huron on out to a sliver of land floating halfway to the other side of the state. An in-between of ideologies—those carried down from the original settlers of the area and those of the new guard. Men like Hendrik, with twisted views of what it meant to be happy.

"You knew them," she whispered to Kirk.

"Yes. In a different life, I knew them."

"You grew up on the Island, and then what? You ran off to join the friars?" She was still confused about Kirk's life's timeline.

"After high school, I went to college and studied psychology, just like I told you. I remained a devout Catholic through it all, just as my parents had been. We all were back then, here on the Island."

This comforted Cadence only minimally. Religious faith and goodness carried less weight in her mind after finding out what a Christian man like Hendrik was capable of.

She couldn't help but to say as much out loud. "What does it mean to be Christian, anyway? Or Catholic? Even devout?"

"Being Christian is a verb. One isn't a Christian unless he or she acts so. But, even when that's true, another truth has the power to trump it."

"What's that?"

"Forgiveness."

"I can't forgive Hendrik." She turned to face Kirk. "He killed his wife."

CHAPTER 37

Hendrik and Katarina had left on the final session, Dr. Kirk Sanders, or Brother as they called him, hadn't known what to do. He'd come to care deeply for Katarina and started to see her as a friend as much as a wife who'd come to him in spiritual need.

Before Hendrik had appeared in the doorway at that last moment, during their embrace, Kirk had planned to show Katarina how she could become more involved in the church. He was going to give her a roadmap to annulment and a custody plan that could work for everyone and then a guide to entering into the lay clergy for now. Maybe one day, she'd become a nun and make something more of the little priory house at the monastery.

It could all still happen, but the next day Kirk saw the couple at mass with their children in tow, three beautiful Dutch girls who adored their father and seemed cold toward their mother.

During doughnuts and coffee in the family center, Hendrik approached Kirk.

"We've reported you," he said, low and gruff.

"Reported who?"

"The Friars. You were grooming my wife. For what, I don't even want to know. I'd warn you to leave her alone, but support for your little establishment out there on the coast will dissolve as soon as the truth comes to light."

Kirk wasn't scared of him. "And what truth is that, Hendrik?" He may be a man of God, but that didn't mean Kirk couldn't stand up to a bully. All the more reason to, in fact. Besides, Kirk never had stood up to Hendrik when they were in school together. Even when Rip complained that his older brother could be a real pill. Back then, Kirk had chalked it up to spoiled-kid syndrome. He hadn't realized the problem was much, much worse. That Hendrik tried to control Rip as much as he tried to control his wife now.

"The truth that you were groping my wife in the privacy of a marriage retreat setting. The truth that you're a nutjob who couldn't hack it in the real world, so you turned to the church. The fact that you're a desperate man with a fake degree," he spat.

"I wasn't groping her. I was comforting her. She's not happy, Hendrik."

"I guess that means your little retreat is ineffective. All the more reason for that place to fold in like cheese in a frittata." He laughed, and it came out light and happy, making it all the more cruel.

Kirk excused himself from Hendrik's presence and threw away the last quarter of his doughnut. The remainder of the little post-mass breakfast, Kirk kept an eye on Katarina, who did a poor job of pretending everything was fine. She practically ignored the children. Didn't take a bite of her doughnut, and barely sipped her coffee.

At one point, he watched her get up to use the restroom, which was at the far side of the family center, back past the kitchen.

Kirk dipped over to the custodial closet which led into the opposite end of the kitchen. He jogged through it in his robe, cursing the garment for its inefficiency, but managed to meet her before she opened the ladies room door. "Katarina," he whispered, his eyes darting down the short hall to ensure no one came their way.

She looked at him sadly, like he was a reminder of some hurt.

"Listen, get the girls and come to the monastery tomorrow after lunch. I'll have it ready for you. You can stay there, in secret."

Her face contorted into confusion. "What? You think I should run away?"

Put that way, it sounded extreme and even dangerous. "Not run away, but...well, I think you should take heed of him. You two need a break."

"A break doesn't mean stealing the girls away to a nunnery."

"That's fair." His breath turned short. He couldn't keep her much longer.

Katarina's face relaxed. "Listen, Brother. Hendrik and I will be fine. I'm not running from him. I'm safe. The girls are, too. This whole thing is not about Hendrik or even our marriage. It's about me."

"You matter," he whispered.

"Thank you. But I can handle it. I can make it work. And one day, I'll come looking for you. And we'll start that nunnery together. Or—" she smiled, a genuine smile that settled his heart and even his mind. "What was it you called it? The abbey house?"

"The priory house." He smiled back, satisfied just then that everything would work. That Hendrik was bluffing about having reported him, and satisfied that Katarina was safe and that she could withstand a marriage to a moody, possessive man. Before she went into the restroom and he left the breakfast to return home, he added, "But I like the abbey house better."

CHAPTER 38—DARLA

Once Darla made it upstairs, she found Mila tickling the boys. She was so good with children.

"You're going to make a great teacher one day," Darla told her.

Mila looked up and smiled. "Just like you. And Mom."

It was preciously endearing that despite everything, Mila had adopted Cadence as her real mother. Even in the face of learning that Katarina hadn't left them, Mila didn't go back on her affections for the woman who came into her life and filled it with happiness.

That was Mila, Darla knew. She was a good girl. A girl with a heart big enough to fit two people in one role. Heart big enough to thwart conflict and big enough to *love*.

Mila looked past Darla. Someone else had followed her in.

"Hi Mr. Acton," Mila said. Then she kissed each boy and stood up. "I'd better go back down to my sisters. I'll leave you two alone."

Once she was gone, Mason settled on the floor and rested on one elbow. He was surprisingly comfortable with the babies, and this gave Darla a quiet, inner thrill. "You were saying, before we came up, that it was strange that Hendrik could kill one wife and be kind to the next."

She looked at him. "Yeah. I don't know. It's something that Cadence will take a while to get over, I guess."

"The police said it was probably an accident, though. Right? That forensics made room for the potentiality that Katarina fell."

"There wasn't a fight. That's true. Maybe he shoved her. But regardless of how it happened, he left her there to rot. And kept it secret. And he went on to live that lie until he died."

"I'm sure it was a hard lie to live with. Maybe he treated Cadence well out of remorse. And the girls, he took good care of them."

"That's true, too. I don't know what to make of it, other than the fact that our family is now mired in this scandal. It's a good thing we decided to let go of the whole venue idea. We'd have never gotten past the rumors and gossip that we were cursed, somehow."

"What will you do with the middle boardwalk house?"

"Rent it, once the funeral is over. It'll be good extra income, and Cadence is willing to let me manage it and take the money until I can find something else."

"Do you want to find another job? I thought you were going to stay home."

"I want to teach. I'll go back, eventually. When the time and the position is right."

"I know of an opening. At our school. We've got a long-term sub in there now, but it's open for the new school year."

"It'll still be too soon. Next year, I'll still want to be home. The boys are babies."

"You could teach at home with this position," Mason replied.

"What?" she looked at him skeptically. "It's a high school position, right?"

"With the way the world is going, the district is

making some big changes. They want to offer college credits, but they can only do it remotely."

"Remotely?"

"Yep. You can stay home and build lessons from your computer. Keep the live lessons short. Grade at home. Everything. I told Tatum about it a while back."

"She never told me."

"She said you weren't ready, I didn't realize she assumed it was an in-person position."

"She probably also figured I didn't want to be too close to you." Darla didn't mean to admit this, but there it was, out on the floor. The truth.

He looked hurt. "You don't?"

"Listen, Mason, the way I feel about you conflicts with my life right now."

"The boys. You don't want to bring men around. I understand that."

"You do?"

"Of course, I do. My Aunt Nora was that way. She kept her personal life private when my Uncle Wendell left. You'd never have known that she saw other men. It came out later, as a little post-mortem scandal all its own. But she did it. She dated."

"Oh."

Awkward silence filled the air until Gabe gurgled a giggle.

Darla scooped him up and cradled him against her. "I can't date. These boys are my world, and they deserve my undivided attention." She didn't look at Mason as she continued. "You distract me, Mason."

"I don't want to pressure you, Darla," he said, his voice low. "But can I ask you something?"

"First, let me put them down in their pack 'n' plays." The boys' eyes were heavy and their breathing slow. Mason carried Shep, and Darla carried Gabe. They deposited each baby carefully into his portable sleeper and then left the room, closing the door gently. "I have to go back in there. I can't just leave them."

"I'll go back with you."

"What was it you were going to ask me, Mason?" she looked at him with a challenge in her eyes.

"What if he were still around?"

"Who?" she asked.

"The boys' dad. If he were around, would your attention *not* be a little divided? Isn't that the thing about parenting? Balancing out your attention within the family."

"First of all, Hunter never had my attention. Not like—" her voice fell away as she looked at Mason.

His strong jaw, stubbled stylishly, and his light eyes staring at her and seeing through her and deep into her world. *Understanding* her. *Waiting* for her. "Not like you would."

Their conversation arrested itself as Darla found herself letting Mason slide his hands into the back of her hair and pull her face to his. She let him kiss her.

Then, against all the good judgment and moral high ground she'd established since learning of her pregnancy, Darla kissed Mason back. And it was the most natural feeling in the world. So natural, that she wondered if maybe there could be virtue in one day giving her boys a father. A good man with a good job who loved her and who loved them and who could appreciate that families were typically a messy, broken bunch of people just trying to make it through life together.

CHAPTER 39—CADENCE

Cadence's ire wasn't reserved for Hendrik alone, though. She also felt anger for herself, for not seeing that he was controlling and manipulative. And she was angry at Kirk, too.

He hadn't been honest with her.

Kirk replied to her now, "It'll take time. You loved him. You trusted him. And the girls, he was their father." He looked down. "By all accounts, he was a good father."

Perhaps equally shocking to the revelation that Hendrik had killed Katarina was that Kirk had been their marriage counselor. That his ties to the island stretched far beyond growing up there and going to St. Mary's with every other island kid.

"You didn't intervene?"

"I tried, but ultimately, it was out of my control. Katarina was a curious woman. You must know this. She struggled with having married Hendrik, and she struggled with having children."

"What a shame," Cadence whispered, although it was nothing new. "But she loved her daughters. She didn't leave them on purpose."

"Absolutely not. From what we know, she came out to the monastery, and Hendrik came, too. Maybe he followed her. Maybe they came together to look for more help. But Hendrik had made good on his threat. He reported the monastery to the diocese, and though he didn't give them *my* name specifically, he slammed our brotherhood efficiently enough and with enough financial power to send us to pieces. Once that came to pass, I left the church and broke my vows. I returned to the mainland, met a woman, and we married, and that marriage was damned from the start. It took me all those years to accept that I was living heavily with guilt. I was drowning in it. When we divorced, I knew I had to come back here and pay my penance."

"You looked for me. You found me out."

"Yes and no. I decided to commit myself to helping the island home I'd sacrificed for my own selfish fears. I had reached out to Rip, an old friend.

He brought me up to speed, and as you can imagine, his version of events protected his brother."

"Rip didn't know what Hendrik did."

"That's why his overview of Hendrik and Katarina's history was so believable. It was pure. Rip was entirely innocent of any of that knowledge, and therefore his account was ultimately convincing."

"Didn't you hear that Katarina went missing? Back then? She was on the news, right?" Cadence asked this, even though she was barely aware of the story and she was living on the island. It'd only come to her sharp attention because she had Mila in her class the next year. A full year later.

"No, I didn't know. But to be honest, even if I had known, I probably would have assumed she had run away. It always felt like she was about to. Like she couldn't stand it, being here." He looked up at the house that sat before them.

"But in January, when the remains were discovered, you didn't think it could be her?"

"In fact, I did." He looked at her now, entirely solemn. "I went to the police, and I told them everything I recalled from back then. I told them I never suspected Hendrik of being truly dangerous, and I'd never have suspected him of foul play or Katarina of being the victim of Hendrik. But I often wondered if it was Katarina there, in that horrid grave. You know, that was the little flower bed right outside the attached cottage we called the priory house."

"Priory house?"

"You know, like a convent or an abbey? That's what Katarina once called it. I liked that."

"Abbey house," Cadence murmured back. She liked it, too. And suddenly, she found herself liking Katarina. Loving her, even. It was a confusing feeling.

"What did the police say back then? When you told them what happened between Katarina and Hendrik?"

"I told them what Rip had told me, which is what Hendrik had told him."

"So the lie was passed on, in Hendrik's death. Protecting him, still."

"I guess."

"It feels right."

He looked at her, frowning. "What?"

"That he did this to her. It feels like the truth. I can't imagine a mother doing what we had always thought Katarina had done. And her daughters were so good. Such good girls. It never made sense for them to be the products of a delinquent mother."

"Even delinquent mothers love their children," Kirk said softly.

"That's true." Now Cadence was ashamed. "I'm sorry for sounding judgmental." It occurred to her that talking to Kirk like this, like he was a friend, felt even better than therapy had felt.

Another thought occurred to her. "When I first came to your house, and we learned that you were my doctor and I'd be your patient, weren't you uncomfortable? Didn't you think it could be a conflict of interest, especially in light of developing events at the construction site with Katarina's remains?"

"Yes, and I considered referring you elsewhere."

"Why didn't you?"

"Because I knew that if there was anyone in the world qualified to help you, it would probably be me."

EPILOGUE

The spring and summer turned sharply into fall for the Sageberry sisters.

Tatum's shelter had won five grants, each from a robust source, including one of the universities, an auto factory, and three from various Detroit big businesses. She'd also earned a generous donation from the Hannigans on Heirloom Island, as well as a generous donation from a mystery woman from the small suburban town Harbor Hills. The mystery woman had just lost her precious cat and hoped to see her memory endure on Heirloom Island, where the woman had gone to school as a girl.

Rip and Tatum, bursting forth with affection for each other, opted to elope over the summer. They'd taken off up to Mackinac Island on a whim, saying their vows in an unknown chapel and returning to Heirloom without any fanfare. It was typical Tatum. A fly-by-night kind of gal who followed her heart and was all the more successful for it. As for Rip, he'd struggled with the fractured reminiscences of his brother.

He began to see Dr. Sanders, even though they were pals. It helped him, knowing that Hendrik was cast in his ways but that to every last person, probably even Katarina, he put on a happy, loving face. It was the best sort of closure Rip could hope for, but it was a work in progress.

Tatum was the ultimate help, though. Tatum and the animals. They'd ended up adopting a fair share of the intakes at The Manger House. Rip built an addition, a second barn. But his bigger project was a two-fold contract between Mr. Roger K. Rutherford and Mr. McGee and the St. Mary's of the Isle Catholic School. It was a funny agreement, and the idea had come from none other than Cadence herself.

∿

With the closing of the Katarina story, the new charter had found itself in a pickle. They could continue their operation and finish the build, but they wouldn't open until mid-year or later.

Or, they could give up.

Because they'd already hired five young women, new teachers, they would either have to pay off the teachers or break their contract.

Cadence offered a third option.

"Welcome to The Abbey House!" Cadence greeted cheerfully, as she and Darla stood at the front doors of the middle boardwalk property.

Three new smiling faces replied eagerly and followed Cadence's direction to enjoy refreshments in the great room before the convocation began.

Darla whispered to her older sister. "This was the neatest idea, Cade."

They grinned at each other and then at Rip and Kirk, who stood just inside of the doors, passing out rooming assignments with Mr. McGee and Mr. Rutherford.

Rip and his crew had taken the middle property and completed a modest addition along the eastside of the property. Three more bedrooms, each with an en suite bathroom. This brought the total number of bedrooms in the middle house to six. Seven, if you counted the expansive den, which they didn't. Not yet, at least.

Mr. Rutherford had been slow to come around, but when Cadence had impressed upon him the idea that his mission and vision for his school were so close to those of St. Mary's, the path was paved.

In just one short month, St. Mary's would reintroduce itself to the island as St. Mary's K-12 School. The school hadn't served secondary grades in ages, and it was about time to make a greater go of the situation.

To support the high school, which would open in phases over time at the location of the in-progress building on the eastern shore, Cadence had the idea to host incoming teachers.

She knew all too well how hard it was to find affordable housing on a small island. Logically, she would give up one of her own properties to help the school.

Tonight, with the arrival of the final three teachers—the ones who'd take on the first ninth grade class—Cadence would unveil the home.

DARLA WAS SET to attend the grand opening of the new teacher housing unit, the house she'd lived in briefly.

Mason would be her date. Of course, he was more than a date.

He was her coworker now, too. Or, he would be once the new school year began. Birch Harbor High had hired Darla to teach their Intro to Humanities with an Emphasis on Fine Arts, remotely, from the comfort of her home. She'd earn full benefits and a full-time teacher salary, and Darla couldn't be more thrilled.

But Mason wasn't *just* her date *and* her coworker.

That summer, after many lengthy conversations on the topic, they went from zero to sixty.

It wasn't what Darla had expected. She'd expected a slow courtship, wherein she'd go to Mason and never bring him around the boys. They'd date. Eventually, they'd turn exclusive. He'd meet the boys anew, as an important person in their lives.

They'd talked at length about the future, and Darla emphasized to him that she didn't want him to spend time around the boys unless *this* was *it*.

And so, in May, Mason told Darla that he was

serious about her and he wanted them to be serious together.

With Cadence and Tatum's encouragement, Darla agreed, and here they were, packing up the boys together just before joining the festivities next door. Three intense months of courting and getting to know one another. Learning about each other's fears and quirks, interests and hopes.

Mason wore the boys in the carrier while Darla was responsible for the diaper bag.

Mason pointed to the bag, "Did you put the extra outfits in? Just in case?"

She gave him a look. "Of course."

"Extra bottles?"

"Yep."

He patted his back pockets then looked panicked. "And the ring?"

She started to roll her eyes and again say yes. She'd been mothering for nearly a year now.

Then her brain rewound itself. "Wait, what did you say?"

"The ring?" His goofy look fell from his face and he almost appeared as though he felt sick. "I said, the ring."

She swallowed. "What ring."

"Your ring."

Darla's hand froze on the side of the diaper bag, where she'd been patting it down for the supplies he'd asked her about.

Mason and the boys moved two steps toward her and he reached around them and to the diaper bag. He slipped his hand into the front pouch, between a pack of diaper wipes and a sleeve of binkies.

A perfect, velvet box slid out, and Mason slowly lowered the three of them to the floor on one of his knees as his arms wrapped around the boys. He opened the box. "Darla Sageberry, will you let me be your children's father?"

She was breathless, but he wasn't done.

"Will you let me be your husband? Darla, will you marry me?"

Her answer was less complicated than his question. She lowered with Mason and her two boys, and she let Mason slide the ring on her finger as she kissed each of them in turn before whispering back through bleary, teary, happy eyes, "*Yes.*"

THE EVENT WAS ROLLING ALONG NICELY, but Cadence still hadn't seen Darla emerge. Tatum had the same observation, and so she sidled up next to her sister. "Where is she?"

"Coming soon, I hope."

"Mason had to talk to her about something," Rip interjected.

Cadence and Tatum exchanged a knowing look. "I thought he was going to wait until the end of this function?" Tatum asked.

"I think it was hard for him to wait. I happen to know the feeling." Rip looped an arm around Tatum's waist.

"Should I start?" Cadence asked fretfully.

"What about Kirk, is he ready?" Rip asked.

Not only were the school leaders and the priest responsible for the new school and today's blessing of the house for the new teachers, but Kirk had agreed to sponsor it heartily. He was funding a monthly stipend for every teacher who would stay at the boardwalk property. His way to welcome them to the island and to honor the charity of the church and help tackle his own demons.

"I'm ready." Kirk appeared near them, dressed neatly in a brown sweater and brown khakis. A cream button-down peeked out from his sweater collar and sleeves, and a beautiful small crucifix hung from his neck. The outfit wasn't all together fashion forward, but Cadence had gifted him the ensemble for tonight's event. It reminded her of what he once was, a Franciscan Monk. Katarina's sole confidant.

"We're here!" Darla and Mason and the boys entered through the door in the nick of time. Darla was beaming and her hand glimmering with a beautiful, simple engagement ring. A string of small diamonds that encircled her delicate finger. At the center, a three stone setting. She showed it off to the others. "It's the trinity set."

"The trinity?" Kirk asked, his interest piqued. "A different trinity symbol."

Mason, proud looking with the twins strapped to his chest, replied, "The past, the present, and the future."

"Ah yes," Kirk replied. "It's beautiful and a great symbol for your love."

The group congratulated Darla and Mason, and Cadence and Tatum revealed he'd asked them for their blessing and had asked her mother, as well, just a month earlier.

It was time for the ceremony to commence, and Cadence and Kirk led the way, hand in hand.

For they were more than a new couple. They

were more than a former therapist and his client. A former monk and a widow.

They were also the official sponsors of the Abbey House, a teacher housing property dedicated to the memory of the woman who'd inadvertently named it: Katarina Van Dam.

It would be there, in The Abbey House, where new teachers could live together in harmony and safety. Where local women could come if they needed refuge for the night—or longer. It would be a home for those who cared for children and loved them, no matter their circumstances. It would be a home for the spirit of the woman who'd loved her husband and her children, but who often wondered where she might go next.

IF YOU ENJOYED THIS SAGA, order Elizabeth Bromke's next sweet romance series, Prairie Creek.

Keep up with the author by joining her newsletter at elizabethbromke.com.

ALSO BY

Heirloom Island:

The Boardwalk House (1)

The Manger House (2)

The Abbey House (3)

Other Series

Prairie Creek

Harbor Hills

Birch Harbor

Hickory Grove

Gull's Landing

Maplewood

ABOUT THE AUTHOR

Elizabeth Bromke writes women's fiction and contemporary romance. She lives in the mountains of northern Arizona with her husband, son, and their sweet dogs, Winnie and Tuesday.

Learn more about the author by visiting her website at elizabethbromke.com.

ACKNOWLEDGMENTS

This book was such a puzzle! After a wacky drafting process that included major additions and changes, I was so lucky to have my trusty editing team help make sure it all pieced itself together properly in the end. A huge thanks to Lisa Lee, Suzanne Brumfield, and Beth Attwood for polishing Cadence's story.

I also wish to thank my dear friends and family, who lend their ears when I'm working through plot points and lend their patience when I check out to spend endless hours alone, just *thinking*. What is a writer without such a terrific support network?

Thank you always to my fabulous readers and ARC team. Sincerely, if it weren't for your ongoing enthusiasm, I'm not sure I'd be writing books at all. All of my stories are for you.

And my boys, Ed and Eddie—thank you for tolerating me through such a crazy writing schedule this time around! I love you to the moon and back!

Made in the USA
Middletown, DE
10 June 2022

66948912R00146